THE NEW EXPERTS

EXPERTS

WIN TODAY'S NEWLY EMPOWERED CUSTOMERS AT THEIR 4 DECISIVE MOMENTS

ROBERT H. BLOOM

GREENLEAF
BOOK GROUP PRESS

Published by Greenleaf Book Group Press
Austin, Texas
www.gbgpress.com

Distributed by Greenleaf Book Group LLC

For ordering information or special discounts for bulk purchases, please contact Greenleaf Book Group LLC at PO Box 91869, Austin, TX 78709, 512.891.6100.

Design and composition by Greenleaf Book Group LLC
Cover design by Greenleaf Book Group LLC

Cataloging-in-Publication data (Prepared by The Donohue Group, Inc.)

Bloom, Robert H.
   The new experts : win today's newly empowered customers at their 4 decisive moments / Robert H. Bloom. -- 1st ed.

   p. ; cm.
ISBN: 978-1-60832-024-0

1. Consumers--Decision making. 2. Consumer behavior. 3. Customer relations. 4. Relationship marketing. I. Title.

HF5415.32 .B568 2010
658.8343   2010922759

Part of the Tree Neutral™ program, which offsets the number of trees consumed in the production and printing of this book by taking proactive steps, such as planting trees in direct proportion to the number of trees used: www.treeneutral.com.

TreeNeutral®

Printed in the United States of America on acid-free paper

10 11 12 13 14   10 9 8 7 6 5 4 3 2 1

First Edition

TO MY WIFE, HARVI, WHO GAVE ME CONFIDENCE
WHEN I WANTED IT AND NEEDED IT, AND CRITICISM
WHEN I DIDN'T WANT IT BUT NEEDED IT—
WITH MY LOVE AND GRATITUDE.

CONTENTS

FOREWORD

Verne Harnish
Founder and CEO, Gazelles, Inc.; author, *Mastering the Rockefeller Habits*; founder, Entrepreneurs' Organization (EO)

The three a.m. nightmare . . .

As this book goes to press, business leaders around the world continue to face sleepless nights, challenged by a prolonged, irregular economic recovery and an ever-changing marketplace. The nightmare they face: growth.

Now more than ever, we seek practical advice about managing and growing our companies—wisdom born from experience in the business trenches that can be translated into action immediately, easily, and affordably. As the leader of a firm that brings new ideas to business leaders around the globe, I have chosen to write this foreword because I believe that *The New Experts* has been written for this pivotal moment in time when we are experiencing a seismic market shift.

Bob Bloom, as always, uses his gift for looking around the corner, simplifying the complex, and employing everyday language. He has identified the yet-unrevealed fundamental problem businesses face right now—how to capture the newly empowered and intensely narcissistic customer—a prospective buyer who has immense choice in every category of goods and services.

In his timely book, Bob focuses on this profound revolution in customer behavior—the emergence of radically changed customers he calls "the new experts." He provides a realistic solution to this universal problem—a down-to-earth solution that can be implemented by business leaders of every kind and size who have the vision and the will to educate and train their organization to win this supremely confident new customer.

Bob explains how to convert prospects into customers and customers into repeat buyers and then into brand advocates. He shows readers how to capture new customers—even today's empowered customers—at the four moments when they are most vulnerable. He demonstrates how to secure customers when they are obsessed with their "pain point"—their yet-unrealized "ambitious dream" or their persistent "three a.m. nightmare."

It was a three a.m. nightmare I faced a few months ago when looking for a place for my family to live in Barcelona. After emailing a few agents recommended to me by a couple colleagues and getting no real results, I woke up startled in the middle of the night, realizing we were moving soon but had no home. So I took control of the process. I jumped on the Internet right then, evaluated several prospective housing options along with some new agents (purely based on their websites), and had a flat leased within twenty-four hours. And I had more information, including a video walkthrough of the property, than the agency that ultimately handled the paperwork.

My wife had a similar situation in ordering our two-year-old some shoes (she often wakes up in the middle of the night realizing she forgot to do this or that). After thoroughly researching her options, she called one of the online retailers with a few questions. When it finally came time to order, Julie requested a certain color, which the customer service rep said wasn't an option. Julie then proceeded to give him the specific product number for that color. Again, the customer knew more than the company's associate.

If you sense this kind of behavioral change in yourself and your customers, you realize how increasingly difficult it is to persuade these radically changed customers to buy from you—not from your hungry competitors—and you recognize that your company's growth is dependent on your willingness to champion change in your business.

If you want to win customers, retain them, and convert them into repeat customers and advocates, you will benefit greatly from reading every page of Bob Bloom's remarkable new book, *The New Experts*.

INTRODUCTION

Most business leaders believe that their current unsatisfactory financial performance is chiefly a result of the recent and current harsh economic realities and the birth of powerful new global competitors. These problems, while severe, are masking a far more enduring problem. Many companies will not thrive—or survive—in the coming years because all businesses are suffering from a more serious and enduring problem that has hidden beneath our former prosperity and our current troubles.

This problem—namely, the upheaval in the fundamental buyer-seller equation—was concealed by the recent boom years during which sellers could sell anything to buyers who were eager to buy everything they could—or as it turned out, could not—afford. The excesses of yesterday—irrational investments, extravagant lifestyles, unwarranted business expansion, and abundant financial results—obscured the emergence of the buyer's newfound power and authority.

Businesses—of every size and type—have been, are now, and will continue to be impacted by this monumental *revolution in buyer behavior.*

Today's buyers—empowered by the Internet, assured by the enormous choice in every segment of commerce, and capitalizing on the acute vulnerability of sellers struggling in this new selling climate—have taken control of the entire purchase progression.

Here are just two startling examples of the results of this monumental alteration of customer behavior:

- In 2009, only 20 percent of car buyers were brand loyal, compared to 80 percent in the 1980s, according to CNW Marketing Research (Bill Vlasic, "For Car Buyers, the Brand Romance Is Gone," *New York Times*, October 20, 2009).

- In 2009, only 36 percent of business travelers claimed that they were brand loyal, compared to 42 percent in 2007, according to Forrester Research ("In Pursuit of Loyalty, *New York Times*, December 1, 2009).

In my forty-five-year career in domestic and international marketing, I learned that growth is the most universal problem in business. But growth is only possible if marketers and sellers can persuade newly informed and assertive customers to buy from them, and that is becoming increasingly difficult to do. Today, in speeches and workshops around the world, I help business leaders create growth strategies that confront the profound change in customer behavior, because I view this development as the most dangerous situation that businesses have ever experienced.

The New Experts focuses entirely on this complex problem, and it delivers a practical, inexpensive solution for generating business growth in this hostile selling environment.

What This Book Can Do for You

If you want to increase your sales to customers who are fully informed about the products and services they want to buy; who are armed with comparative data about quality, availability, and price; and who are determined to be successful on their terms, you will gain fresh insights from *The New Experts. It offers simple explanations, illuminating examples, and realistic solutions.*

If you want to learn how to improve your prospect-to-customer conversion; how to recruit and retain customers with little or no investment in advertising or infrastructure; and how to generate repeat purchase, advocacy, and referral from customers, you will benefit from this book. *You will grow your revenue and profits.*

If you want to emerge from this disastrous recession ready to prosper from the improving economy, you will benefit from this book.

Here is the path that I will lead you on—the path to greater sales with less investment and more profitable growth.

- In Chapter 1, I offer a brief but revealing analysis of the biggest challenge facing businesses today: the profound shift in the buyer-seller equation. I explain why you must learn to think like a customer rather than a seller or suffer the consequences of the radical change in buyer behavior.

- In Chapter 2, you will discover why you have only four chances—4 Decisive Customer Moments—to make your business 1st choice. I identify the pitfalls at each of the four perilous moments in the purchase progression and explain how you can protect your prospects and customers from hungry competitors.

- In Chapter 3, I define the critical element of Customer Preference—the X factor that will enable you to influence and win customers at each of the 4 Decisive Customer Moments. And I explain how you can avoid costly "customer churn."

- In chapters 4 through 7, I explain the nature of each of the four moments, how you can create enduring Customer Preference, and how to leverage the Customer Preference you've developed to generate highly profitable repeat purchase, advocacy, and referrals.

With the practical knowledge, actionable tips, and numerous relevant and diverse cases in the chapters that follow, you will learn how to turn your biggest challenge into a business-building advantage for your brand or company. You will learn how to make your business 1st choice over all your competitors.

1

THE REVOLUTION IN
BUYER BEHAVIOR

Buyers no longer care who they buy from.

This revolution in buying habits did not happen suddenly. No one could have anticipated, however, that this change would occur during the long period when sellers were *in control of the purchase progression*—of products, of credit, of information, and even of when, where, and how products could be purchased. Sellers controlled every aspect of the buyer-seller relationship—so why should anyone have doubted their power?

When sellers were in control, retailers, not credit or debit cards, were the only source of credit for the goods and services you wanted. Retailers dictated the terms under which you could purchase goods from them, and it was difficult to shop around for better terms elsewhere because, if better terms could be found, the approval process was often lengthy and complex—sellers were the primary influence in your credit decisions.

When sellers were in control, car dealerships, not the Internet, were the only places buyers could obtain information about the cool convertibles they desired. Car dealers controlled what you knew and, more important, limited your access to what they did not want you to know—sellers were the primary influence in your purchasing decision.

When sellers were in control, buyers who were desperate for cash over a long holiday weekend when their banks were closed did without cash; there were no ATMs just around the corner. Banks determined where, when, and how you were able to gain access to your own money—sellers were the primary influence in your financial decisions.

Today, buyers are in control.

This reversal of supremacy has placed every business around the globe in a perilous situation.

If you do not believe this fundamental shift in the buyer-seller equation has occurred, this book will change your mind. I will explain why this inverted equation has created a revolution in buyer behavior, why this behavioral change is having a serious effect on your business, how to avoid the pitfalls that occur when you underestimate the power your customers now wield, and how to make the most of the influence you can wield at the right moments in the lengthy purchase progression.

*This book will deliver a solution—it will
enable you to make your business 1st choice.*

The solution is to master the four moments when customers
are most easily influenced either to buy from you or to move on
to buy from one of your competitors. The first step is to understand the transformation of your buyer.

How Buyers Took Control

Suddenly, or so it seemed, technology came to the aid of
buyers.

Technology enabled customers to become better and more
quickly informed, and sellers, eager to capitalize on the newly
informed buyers, gave them more and more choices. Sellers
offered buyers new options—sizes, colors, methods, flavors,
packaging, hours of operation, styles, and terms. Responding to
the demand for more information and more points of comparison, sellers provided new ways to access their products: multiple
locations; 800 numbers that facilitated 24/7 purchase, and websites that could be accessed from anywhere and at any time, sites
that delivered gobs of valuable information about products and
services. Buyers then had a vast number of venders from which
to choose, as well as access to technology that could help them
assess their many new options.

*This confluence of technology and choice
started customer loyalty down the slippery
slope—ultimately, customer loyalty died.*

Technology and choice changed every aspect of commerce, but *the transformation in the marketplace went largely unnoticed.* A robust economy created an expanding middle class that had access to easy credit and expanding discretionary income. Businesses experienced rapid domestic growth and discovered that customers in all corners of the world were hungry for the ever-broader array of products they manufactured and the ever-wider variety of services they provided. Sellers didn't have to work to sell their goods and services, because buyers were buying everything in sight. And sellers didn't realize that the underlying change in buyer behavior was having a profound effect on their businesses, because initially, they were benefiting from the change.

Technological innovation made buying easier, faster, simpler, and cheaper. Search engines enabled customers to compare everything, including the biggest game-changer of all—price. Yahoo, Google, and mobile devices of every kind gave buyers knowledge and authority instantly, and they wielded them to get the lowest price possible. Facebook and Twitter connected millions of customers with millions of sellers, and millions of sellers with millions of customers—in real time. Price and options became the most critical factor in determining where and when to buy—the death knell for customer loyalty.

Disagree? Consider these facts:

According to a December 18, 2009, *New York Times* article, "Powerful software applications for devices like Apple iPhone are making it easy for bargain-hunting consumers to see if another retailer is offering a better deal . . . and use it to haggle at the cash register." Retailers are doing their best to take advantage of these changes in behavior by redesigning their sites to make them more accessible to mobile browsers and sending coupons to customers via their cell phones (Claire Cain Miller, "Mobile Phones Become Essential Tool for Holiday Shopping"). But they can't change the fact that customers are more knowledgeable about competitors' prices and about the products these customers are considering.

As mentioned in the Introduction, according to a recent study by CNW Marketing Research, only one in five car buyers stayed loyal to a brand in 2009. Compare that to the 1980s when almost four out of five customers bought the same brand (Bill Vlasic, "For Car Buyers, the Brand Romance Is Gone," *New York Times*, October 20, 2009). Art Spinella, CNW's president, proclaimed, "There really isn't any brand loyalty anymore." And according to James Farley, Ford Motor Company's head of marketing, "Brand loyalty has shrunk because of widespread improvements in the products." People have more and better options, and they know all about them.

Writing on Forbes.com/CMO Calculus, in a piece called "Is Customer Loyalty Dead?" marketing guru Mike Linton advises companies to acknowledge this "new world order" among buyers: "An auto salesperson recently explained that he had lost a sale after three meetings and numerous calls, because the customer used the Internet to find the same car for $100 less ten miles away" (August 28, 2009).

Unlike Frankenstein, customer loyalty will not rise from the grave that was dug by a robust economy, abundant choice, and seller apathy. Search engines presided over customer loyalty's funeral and empowered buyers to take control of their entire buying experience. Here's the brutal reality of the revolution in buyer behavior:

Buyers no longer care which seller they buy from—which gives buyers all the power.

Here's why:

- Buyers know all too well that their favorite search engine will instantly connect them to dozens of seller sites where they can compare every aspect of the choices they are offered.

- Buyers know that they will find the best value somewhere in the marketplace because the marketplace is full of options.

- Buyers are empowered by the reality that they are in control.

Recently, my son needed a new battery for his off-brand laptop and found plenty of sellers on eBay. He got his new battery for $40 from a seller in China rather than buying a battery in the $150 range from the several domestic sites he visited. My son and all the other buyers in the world are aware of the vast array of options now available to them. Is it any wonder that *most buyers no longer care where or what brand they buy?*

Choice is why buyers fell out of love with loyalty and in love with options. The abundance of options in the world, in your category, and in your neighborhood is why you must make your business 1st choice.

But buyers do care about fulfilling their needs and making the best purchase decision—and that is how you can win them over at four critical customer moments.

Sellers Can Still Win Customers

Buyers—every human being on this planet, including you—have wants, needs, and aspirations as well as apprehensions, concerns, and fears. These emotional forces—whether positive or negative—drive our purchase decisions.

- The couple *wants* a sleek new BMW convertible to give them pleasure, feed their egos, get them to their destination in style, and reward them for their hard work.

- Our company *needs* a larger crane so that we can win bigger projects, enhance our firm's reputation, and accelerate our growth.

- We have *aspirations* for our family. Our daughter has the talent to be a gifted pianist, so we want to send her to the best music schools and buy her the finest piano.

- The couple has *apprehensions* about walking into a jewelry store to buy a diamond ring because, despite their extensive learning online, they are still unsure of their ability to evaluate or affirm the quality of the mysterious, expensive, and highly desired objects called diamonds.

- Managers voice their *concerns* about choosing and installing a new technology system for their firm because it may not function properly, may end up costing too much, and may become obsolete overnight.

- We wake up in the middle of the night because of our *fears* that the heavy equipment we are shipping halfway around the world will not arrive on schedule or will be damaged en route.

As buyers, we experience emotional impulses such as these much of the time. At these individual and personal buyer moments, our wants, needs, and aspirations and our apprehensions, concerns, and fears motivate us—often compel us—to purchase goods and services. When this appetite to buy is at its strongest, we are impulsive and vulnerable.

This urge to buy is the moment that we, the buyers, can be most easily influenced by a persuasive seller—convinced that this is the seller to buy from and confident that this is the moment to buy.

Yet we, the sellers, do not understand that this momentary opportunity to regain control exists, nor do we know how to capitalize on it.

Buyers are most responsive to a seller's influence when powerful emotions force buyers' decision making—when buyers are in the process of purchasing something important to them. That something important can be expensive and vital, such as a new fleet of trucks, or inexpensive and seemingly unessential, such as a fresh bouquet of flowers for Mom on Mother's Day. Both purchases—the trucks and the flowers—are important to the buyer at that crucial moment when he has an intense desire to purchase.

But you must remember that buyers, while momentarily vulnerable, are still in control of the lengthy purchase progression. Buyers know that they will find products or services to meet their wants, needs, and aspirations—and sellers to provide the customer assistance, delivery, and warranty that will reduce their apprehensions, concerns, and fears.

Unfortunately, most sellers do not understand how the recently transformed buyers think and feel in these moments. Most sellers have forgotten how critical these vulnerable customer moments are to them, as sellers. Most sellers do not realize that these are the moments to make the most of their influence over their potential customer.

These emotionally driven purchasing events are *the* Decisive Customer Moments—the vulnerable and impulsive customer moments when you can most easily induce the buyer to choose your firm over your competitors. All businesses have 4 Decisive Customer Moments—four fleeting opportunities when they can make their firm 1st choice and beat out their competitors. To capitalize on these four decisive moments, sellers must change the way they think and act. I will pinpoint these precious moments for you and explain how you can use them to increase revenue, improve profitability, and grow your business.

First you must understand the key to your success as a seller in this era when buyers are in control of the purchase progression: At these fragile moments, the seller must think like a buyer.

Sellers Must Think Like Buyers

Sellers—you and all the sellers on this planet—are driven by many of the same human forces that buyers are driven by, but you, like all sellers, have a single, compelling goal that feeds those emotions: You just want to succeed and prosper.

That's why you have an intense need to sell your customer that cool BMW, that giant crane, that superb piano, that diamond jewelry, that complex new technology system, or that shipping service to move heavy equipment.

To achieve our ambition to succeed and prosper, we sellers want customers and potential customers to

- admire our brand,
- click on our site before any competitors' sites,
- remember our location,
- use our services exclusively, and
- believe that we offer a better value than our competitors.

Yesterday, these expectations might have been reasonable. Today, these expectations are unrealistic. Sellers must stop thinking that buyers of industrial goods, consumer products, or services care about how long the sellers have been in business, how many offices they have, how dedicated their employees are, and how attractive and sincere their CEO is.

That is "seller think" and "seller talk"—buyers do not care about most seller attributes and are turned off by seller hyperbole.

Too many sellers bombard you, the buyer, with trite, unbelievable, undistinguishing, and insulting buyer-centric slogans that typically start with "we."

- "We are dedicated to you."
- "We have a passion to serve you."
- "We are committed to your future."
- "We are the greenest company in the world."
- "We will beat everyone's price."

And, of course, we've all heard phony-sounding words that seem all too similar to actual slogans, such as, "We are the most honest, the most pure, and the most reliable company in the universe."

Buyers care about the seller's quality, reliability, and responsiveness; they do not care about the seller's inflated promises. Miele, the marketer of high-quality major household appliances, clearly understands this. When you call most sellers, a robotic voice commands you to "listen closely, as our options have changed" and then puts you into a holding queue while you wait to talk to somebody who has little relatable experience with the product. Miele, on the other hand, responds to homemakers' desperate calls for help by dispatching a well-informed homemaker or a salaried technician or both to help owners of Miele products in their kitchens and living rooms.

The Miele part-time employee—who uses the products in her own home and is further trained to handle minor problems with them—explains how some minor adjustments can solve the dishwasher's drainage problems. Along the way, she also ever so gently offers ideas about loading the customer's dishwasher to avoid breakage and save energy. Just think how this pleasant, solution-oriented experience positively affects the buyer's feelings about Miele and confidence about the brand she chose.

Buyers do not care about sellers' advertisements, websites, or 800 numbers unless or until these media facilitate the buyers' satisfaction or fulfillment.

Wal-Mart has become 1st choice for millions upon millions of customers. If you want to know the company's secret, read and then reread this simple advice from Eduardo Castro-Wright, vice chairman of Wal-Mart Stores, in the *New York Times*: "Think about the way that you yourself would act, or do act, as a customer" (Adam Bryant, "Corner Office," May 23, 2009).

Break Out of Seller-Think to Survive

So start thinking like your potential buyer right this minute. Turn off your "seller's brain" and turn on your "buyer's brain." For the next few paragraphs, *forget you are a seller—become a buyer and think like a buyer.*

You, *the buyer,* are cyber connected to other buyers via Facebook, today's ultimate connector; Twitter, the rapidly growing micro-blogging service; and many other social networking sites. Facebook has more than 250 million members, signs new members at the rate of a million a day, and is translated into forty languages. More than 120 million people log on to Facebook each day to connect with their self-defined "tribe," and these potential buyers spend a combined 5 billion minutes a day on the site. Facebook's fastest-growing segment is thirty-five-year-olds and up, 80 percent of the biggest U.S. advertisers use it, and it helped put Obama in the White House. Facebook recognizes the phenomenal business opportunity it has in its grasp and is transforming itself into a commercial destination for online shopping. Businesses that don't capitalize on social media's power will be beaten out of their markets eventually.

You, *the buyer*, are connected to blogs, email, online newsletters, buyer's guides, and consumer reports. You are exceptionally well informed and enjoy sharing information about your buying experiences—good experiences and bad.

You, *the buyer*, now enjoy and benefit from going online to compare every aspect of the purchase you intend to make, online or off. A few clicks and you know more about the products and services you are considering than many of those whose job it is to facilitate your purchase, for example:

- The language-challenged telephone salesperson located offshore

- The part-time clerk or the eager yet inexperienced kid behind the counter

- The untrained "sales associate"

- The unmotivated manager or maître d' standing near the door trying to look very busy but doing nothing to help customers

You, *the buyer*, click on Amazon.com in the comfort of your home and discover the wealth of information offered about a book you are interested in. Therefore, why would you stand in line at the help desk of a giant bookstore chain, only to find that the well-meaning but clueless customer assistance manager is unable to tell you anything about the book you may want to buy? Maybe—just maybe—this is why so many neighborhood bookstores have gone out of business and why the book chains are suffering. Maybe this is why Amazon is thriving.

Jeff Bezos, founder and CEO of Amazon, is really in touch with the buyer behavior revolution; he believes that the success his firm has enjoyed is powered by the way Amazon thinks about customers. His comment in the *New York Times* says it all: "We start with customers, figure out what they want, and figure out how to get it to them" (Joe Nocera, "Put Buyers First? What a Concept," January 5, 2008).

That attitude has led to Amazon's tremendous growth in the twenty-first century as a general retailer that proactively "[nudges] loyal customers to buy a greater variety of products by offering free shipping and speedy delivery with clubs like the $79-a-year Amazon Prime" (Brad Stone, "Can Amazon Be the Wal-Mart of the Web?" *New York Times*, September 20, 2009).

Do you know what your customers want,
and are you giving it to them?

Of course, you and I are both buyer and seller. Although most of us make a living selling something, each of us buys products and services for ourselves or our company or someone we care for. When we do so, we are as unfaithful and selfish as any buyer out there, looking for the best deal and walking away from our previous relationships with former sellers of choice. When we assume our role as a seller, however, we become obsessed with our selling task: We forget how we, as buyers, live, work, play, think, and act.

Far too often, we, as sellers, think like a seller and act like a seller.

For example, Coke thinks like a seller. As a result, Coke has lost its once indomitable image in the beverage category. Coke just wants to sell buyers a product, so Coke keeps telling buyers about Coke's taste. But every buyer already knows what Coke tastes like. More important, none of us walks around thinking about taste—we are totally focused on our lives.

Coke needs to start thinking like a buyer again. The Coke brand must crawl into the buyer's head in those moments when the buyer is working and playing—when the buyer is focused on her personal needs and desires. We might be motivated to buy more Coke at those vulnerable moments when we crave a Coke after too many hours at the computer, when we want to chill out with friends over Coke and pizza in the park, or when we have a Coke celebration with our kids after a soccer win.

"Wait," you say, "Coke is big, rich, and powerful; why does an iconic brand like Coke have to think like a buyer?" No company or brand—even the famous ones—can any longer rely on the dearly departed customer loyalty.

Coke has to think like a buyer because its consumer is rapidly shifting to natural beverages like juices and water. Coke has to think like a buyer because Pepsi is an aggressive competitor whose imaginative marketing appeals to the soft drink buyer's emotions. However, Coke also has to contend with—think like—another buyer who is central to Coke's very existence. Supermarkets, big boxes, and large drug chains, like all buyers today, are in control of the sale—they negotiate harder, expect more, and offer less. Coke's retail customer acts like the powerful buyer it is by displaying the higher-priced Coke and Pepsi right next to its lower-priced private label cola. Confronted with these opponents, Coke has an urgent need to think like a buyer in order to get its product in front of consumers and to recruit and retain soft drink buyers at this pivotal stage in its life cycle.

Like Coke, Microsoft is another iconic seller that is so rich and successful, it could easily be complacent, like many other large (and small) sellers. But in contrast to Coke, this smart marketer consistently works hard to think like a buyer, because it faces numerous challenges that threaten its dominance and very existence. Governments everywhere are trying to destroy Microsoft's perceived hold over users by initiating legal action against its products or attempting to break up the firm. Google and ambitious technology start-ups are introducing new products that could dethrone Microsoft because it's one of the world's few remaining sellers that remain in control.

Microsoft knows that tech vendors, tech retailers, and tech users have a great deal of pent-up hostility toward the firm, a common outlook toward such powerful companies. Yes, Microsoft could rest on its lofty position, but unlike Coke, the firm aggressively and intelligently protects its prominence by launching new products, such as Bing, its new search engine that attempts to deliver results faster than Google does. Microsoft thinks like its users by offering helpful hints, inviting questions, and providing solutions *while its users are online—while users want and need shortcuts or instant solutions.* Microsoft publishes and updates user manuals, offers customers help through hotlines, and requires that technicians who service Microsoft users go through rigorous certification programs. Moreover, the company consistently introduces new technology to assure that users have reason after reason to stay with the brand.

Microsoft's approach to customer continuity may sound obvious, but all of us own and use technology products and services that promise to help us but often do not deliver. New technologies might damage or destroy Microsoft, but complacency will not bury the company.

The surest way to become or remain 1st choice is to think like your customers, stay connected to your customers so they want to stay connected to you, and deliver on what you promise your customers.

Every business—regardless of its size, type, or location—needs to think like a potential buyer of its products or services. You can think like your prospects by giving them a reason to look at your business or brand *before looking at your competitors.* Thinking like a buyer will enable you to actively recruit and retain customers so you can grow your business—in any economic environment.

Ask yourself this—can you afford not to think like a buyer?

The Solution That Changes the Rules

Your solution to the revolution in buyer behavior—to your need for profitable growth—is to think like a buyer at your 4 Decisive Customer Moments.

At each of your Decisive Customer Moments, you can influence your prospective customers when they are most vulnerable and impulsive—you can motivate them to choose you over your competitors.

At each of your Decisive Customer Moments, you can consider your prospective customers' perspective—you can think like a buyer—and do what is necessary to fulfill their wants, needs, and aspirations and to allay their apprehensions, concerns, and fears.

At each of your Decisive Customer Moments, you can persuade your prospective customer to choose your company over your competitors.

At each of these crucial moments, you
can make your business 1st choice.

You just need to understand when those decisive moments are occurring and what it will take to influence your customer.

I've devoted the pages in this book to helping companies capitalize on their 4 Decisive Customer Moments, using these moments to recruit and retain customers without risky investment in advertising and infrastructure.

I'll start by explaining when these four moments occur and how they can make all the difference. Then I'll introduce you to the surest path to succeed at each of your 4 Decisive Moments— a concept that will help you convert potential customers into enduring customers and enthusiastic advocates for your brand or company. I'll offer a foundational concept that will help you influence customers at each moment. I'll spend the rest of the book exploring these moments in detail, offering practical advice, real-world cases, and cautionary tales that will help you transform how your business thinks and works in this radically changed buyer-dominant era.

If you're ready to discover the power of your Now-or-Never Moment, your Make-or-Break Moment, your Keep-or-Lose Moment, and your Multiplier Moment to grow your sales, your profits, and your business, read on.

Take a Moment to Consider...

whether you are ready to compete in a world where buyers no longer care where they buy.

1. Does your company understand today's technology-empowered buyer?
2. Do you think like your customer does (that is, like a buyer), or do you still think like a seller?
3. Can your firm persuade prospects to choose your business over your competitors?

To create profitable growth, you must be able to think like a buyer and deliver the benefits your buyers want at the 4 Decisive Customer Moments.

2

YOUR 4 DECISIVE
CUSTOMER MOMENTS

A purchase is not when money changes hands. It is not the instant when the register spits out the bill or the moment when the credit card slip is handed to the customer or the ceremonial signing of the long-negotiated construction contract.

Customer purchase is a lengthy progression—
for every kind of product and service
and for purchases of any amount.

A purchase is a progression for the buyer—regardless of whether it is an enormous, long-considered purchase, such as a contract for the construction of a skyscraper, or a small impulse purchase, such as a package of gum at the airport to help spare an earache during takeoff.

A purchase is also a progression for the seller—the transaction is not finished when the last piece of Sheetrock is installed in the skyscraper or when the gum is unwrapped for takeoff. After the skyscraper is complete, the building may require expansion or remodeling. After the plane is in the air, the consumer still wants to enjoy the gum's fresh taste or may desire another taste sensation later in the long, boring flight.

Along the purchase progression, as revealed in Chapter 1, there are occasions that are critical to both buyer and seller. Although the buyer is in control of every step of this purchase progression, there are 4 Decisive Customer Moments when sellers can persuade buyers to purchase from their firm.

The four invaluable occasions in the purchase progression when you can persuade prospects to buy from your firm—and not from your competitors—are, in sequential order:

1. The Now-or Never Moment—your first brief contact

2. The Make-or-Break Moment—the lengthy transaction process

3. The Keep-or-Lose Moment—the customer's continued usage

4. The Multiplier Moment—repeat purchase, advocacy, and referral

You can make your business 1st choice at each of the 4 Decisive Customer Moments.

Decisive Moment #1: Your Now-or-Never Moment

The buyer's all-too-brief first point of contact with your business is your Now-or-Never Moment.

It is impossible to overestimate the importance of your prospects' initial contact with your company. Contacts not converted into customers at your Now-or-Never Moment will vanish—probably forever.

> *Given this reality, why is the contact-to-customer conversion ratio for most businesses so alarmingly low?*

Here are some common responses from business leaders with whom I have discussed this serious seller problem:

- "Initial contacts are unpredictable."

- "It's impossible to prepare for every possibility."

- "You can't win them all."

- "Most of these contacts are just time-wasters."

On rare occasions, I have heard a more candid explanation: "To tell you the truth, I just don't know how to fix my low conversion problem."

In Chapter 4, I will provide you with the specific actions you can take to improve your contact-to-customer conversion ratio at your highly perishable Now-or-Never Moment.

Decisive Moment #2: Your Make-or-Break Moment

The lengthy transaction period between the buyer and your business is your Make-or-Break Moment.

How many times have you heard these "promises" from those responsible for your sales results?

- "It's a done deal."
- "The contact is in the bag."
- "My contact says his boss will sign today."
- "We can stop worrying about this one."

If you are like most business leaders, you never stop worrying about pending sales because you know from experience that far too many transactions fall through at your Make-or-Break Moment, the extended period of consideration, negotiation, and decision to purchase.

I'll bet you've also heard the following "explanations" from your sales team far too often:

- "The buyer got cold feet."
- "The person I'm talking to can't make the final decision."
- "A competitor jumped in from nowhere with a lowball deal."
- "Someone 'upstairs' decided to give the contract to his golfing buddy."

In Chapter 5, I'll identify the specific actions you can take to preserve your hard-earned prospective customer and improve your odds at your perilous Make-or-Break Moment.

Decisive Moment #3: Your Keep-or-Lose Moment

Your Keep-or-Lose Moment is the period when your buyer is actually using your business's products or services.

After they conclude a transaction, most business leaders breathe a sigh of relief and start concentrating all their resources on their next big sales opportunity. Of course, you must pursue new prospects aggressively and continuously, but it is equally important to *nourish and maintain your relationship with a customer while that current customer is using, consuming, enjoying, and relying on the product or service she purchased from you.*

Maintaining performance is essential at your Keep-or-Lose Moment because you will never generate the high-margin repeat purchase, advocacy, and referral you want from this customer unless she

- obtains the benefits you promised,

- receives the problem-solving service you promised, and

- feels just as "loved" after the sale as she did during the selling process.

In Chapter 6, you will discover numerous ways to sustain your favored position with a buyer throughout your Keep-or-Lose Moment.

Decisive Moment #4: Your Multiplier Moment

Your Multiplier Moment is your conversion of a one-time customer into a repeat customer and an advocate and referral source for your company.

Customers' repeat purchases from your firm and enthusiastic recommendations of your firm will *produce transactions that require far less investment* and will *create far more profitable revenue.* This is why your business must sustain its performance long after the completion of the transaction and throughout your pivotal Multiplier Moment.

To assure that your sales bucket is not leaking faster than you can fill it, and to be confident that your profit margins are where they should be, you must have a reliable system of metrics to measure your performance with accuracy.

In Chapter 7, you will learn how to effectively build and use your personal equity in motivating your customers to buy more and to recommend your company to others. You will also learn how to institutionalize, evaluate, and elevate your performance at your precious but precarious Multiplier Moment.

Of course, you have experienced all four of these Decisive Customer Moments—you always knew they were important. However, the purchase progression you previously experienced has radically changed: Your buyers now have immense choice, unlimited access to information about your products or services, and the technology to compare your offer to your competitors' offers. Remember that your buyers no longer care whether they buy from you or from one of your numerous competitors.

Buyers are now in control of your entire purchase progression.

Success at one, two, or even three Decisive Customer Moments is no longer the enduring, profitable success you seek.

Failure to sustain your performance at all 4 Decisive Customer Moments can be a recipe for business failure, as this next illustration proves.

Rise and Fall through 4 Decisive Customer Moments

In 1983, General Motors announced to the world that it would introduce a "different kind of car company" called Saturn. The company's goal—"rethink everything"—was admirable and ambitious.

To help assure that this "different kind of car company" would function differently from other GM brands and deliver what buyers wanted,

- the Saturn operating unit would operate independently from GM;

- the Saturn car would be a revolutionary, new small-car concept built in Spring Hill, Tennessee, not Detroit—the traditional hub of the automotive industry; and

- the Saturn dealers would offer customers a new kind of shopping experience—there would be no haggling over price, long the annoying practice of auto dealers.

Dealers eagerly lined up to become part of the new nationwide dealer network. Everything seemed to be in place for Saturn to establish a successful new automotive selling model and become an iconic example of mastery of every Decisive Customer Moment.

In 1990, *seven long years after the original Saturn announcement*, the first new Saturn car rolled off the assembly line in the all-new Tennessee plant.

To create success at its *Now-or-Never Moment, the vitally important point of first contact*, Saturn launched with an enormously expensive nationwide print and broadcast advertising campaign. Although conventional off-line media was the only option at that time, the campaign created a huge buzz about Saturn all over America, and the automotive press welcomed and endorsed this innovative idea in an industry not known for innovation. The company trained its dealers in "low-pressure" sales methods, and customers flocked to dealers to benefit from this "new kind of shopping experience." The first point of contact with Saturn paid off as thousands of American customers purchased the car of their choice without the traditional haggling routine.

"The promise of Saturn, from its inception, was how it conducted business rather than the specific models it sold . . . [Its] no-haggle, one-price policy took the strain out of negotiating deals, and new buyers were treated like royalty" (Bill Vlasic and Nick Bunkley, "Detroit's Mr. Fix-It Takes on Saturn," *New York Times*, September 19, 2009).

To ensure success at Saturn's *Make-or-Break Moment, the lengthy transaction period between buyer and seller*, Saturn invited customers to witness their own car on the assembly line at the Spring Hill manufacturing facility. Customers, far more numerous than anticipated, traveled long distances to celebrate the "birth of" their Saturn at Spring Hill. The press loved this idea—newspapers and magazines featured photos of the festive event. Local and national TV and radio stations showed grinning customers climbing into their shiny new Saturn right after it rolled off the assembly line, and dealers, inspired by the event, were motivated to follow through on their vital role in the lengthy purchase progression by avoiding the contentious negotiation phase.

Saturn came through with flying colors at its *Keep-or-Lose Moment, the buyer's use of the seller's products and services*, because Saturn's automotive products delivered on performance. Initially, the brand ranked as the highest-quality American car, with defect ratings equivalent to those of Honda and Toyota. Moreover, according to Saturn's history website, *Popular Mechanics* acknowledged Saturn's quality when it gave Saturn a design and engineering award for "manufacturing processes that result in exceptionally high quality for an all-new vehicle." The press was generous in its praise and the car performed for customers, *making Saturn's Keep-or-Lose Moment highly successful.*

At the beginning of Saturn's *Multiplier Moment, when repeat purchase, advocacy, and referral are essential to enduring profitable success*, only Lexus and Infinity surpassed Saturn's high satisfaction ratings. Effective customer communications and community involvement further enhanced Saturn's ability to turn customers into repeat customers and referrals. In the first three years, Saturn sold more than half a million vehicles, *so it appeared that Saturn would be successful at its critical Multiplier Moment.*

All too soon, however, *Saturn found it difficult to continue to succeed at all four of its Decisive Customer Moments* because the excessively long Saturn-to-market timeline allowed competitive car companies from the United States, Asia, and Europe to introduce exciting new entries and new buyer-centric strategies that were equal or superior to Saturn's. Moreover, most new models were upmarket, and Saturn was unprepared to create and market new models that customers found as appealing as the competitors' wide array of impressive new options. Saturn's "rethink everything" concept worked initially, but GM and Saturn failed to anticipate these new developments. Then, Saturn just stopped thinking altogether.

Ultimately, Saturn began to fail because its products and ideas were stuck in a 1980s time warp rather than keeping pace with the radically changed consumer and automotive landscape of the 1990s and early 2000s. To combat this problem, dealers tried to entice customers to buy by using the old, familiar red-tag sales, and they often resorted to conventional haggling to improve their margins.

To make matters worse, GM's overall sales and share, which had been declining for some time, started to deteriorate at an alarming rate. Saturn, originally independent from GM, came under GM's direct control and cost-cutting thumb. Saturn could no longer afford to deliver the tangible and emotional benefits that it promised its customers and that customers wanted and expected at each Decisive Customer Moment.

Without the ability to sustain performance, Saturn's downward spiral accelerated and then buried the once-promising brand that had enjoyed success far too briefly.

In June 2009, nineteen years after its introduction of a "new kind of car company," GM filed for bankruptcy, and shortly thereafter, it closed down the entire Saturn operation, leaving 350 stunned dealers, who had made heavy investments in the Saturn brand, without a brand to sell. Hopes were raised that summer when the highly respected Roger Penske expressed interest in the brand.

Penske Automotive Group took the deal off the table in late September, however, when it couldn't find a partnering auto manufacturer to build vehicles and distribute them under the Saturn brand name. GM's chief executive, Fritz Henderson, immediately released a statement that the company would shut down the Saturn division by 2010: "Today's disappointing news comes at a time when we'd hoped for a successful launch of the Saturn brand into a new chapter. We will be working closely with our dealers to ensure Saturn customers are cared for as we transition them to other G.M. dealers in the months ahead" (Nick Bunkley and Bill Vlasic, "G.M. to Close Saturn After Deal Fails," *New York Times*, September 30, 2009).

The Key to Mastery of Your 4 Decisive Customer Moments

What Saturn was exceptionally good at initially but then could not sustain was creating Customer Preference at each of the 4 Decisive Customer Moments. Customer Preference is your solution to the revolution in buyer behavior—your opportunity to recruit and retain a buyer who no longer cares where he buys.

Creating Customer Preference for your business at each of the 4 Decisive Customer

Moments will make your brand or business 1st choice in the mind of each of your buyers.

To build Customer Preference and take advantage of all the benefits it offers, remember these truths:

- In the mind of your buyer, you don't have to be the biggest in your industry.

- In the mind of your buyer, you don't have to manufacture the best product.

- In the mind of your buyer, you don't have to have the most well-known brand.

- In the mind of your buyer, you don't have to offer a more compelling promise.

- In the mind of your buyer, you don't have to have the biggest marketing budget.

However, in the mind of your buyer, *you do have to deliver a different benefit* from your competitors and *consistently provide that benefit at each Decisive Customer Moment.* This customer-centric way of thinking and acting requires little investment in infrastructure or advertising, but it delivers powerful results to your business.

Delivering a benefit that the customer values will create Customer Preference for your business and make your brand or company the customer's 1st choice.

Customer Preference is the surest path to success at each of the decisive moments. It is the solution that will change the rules in this buyer-dominant climate we sellers live in.

The remainder of this book is about how you can create Customer Preference for your enterprise at each of the 4 Decisive Customer Moments. We will start by gaining a fuller understanding of "preference" and why it is such a powerful weapon to gain traction in the battle to become 1st choice.

Take a Moment to Consider...

whether your business is succeeding at the 4 Decisive Customer Moments.

1. Are you converting prospects into prospective customers at their first point of contact with your business?

2. Are you tired of hearing that "the pending sale fell through" and "a competitor jumped in at the last minute"?

3. Are your products or services meeting the expectations of your customers? Are you measuring performance trends?

4. Can you consistently convert one-time customers into repeat customers, advocates, and referral sources for your company?

5. To succeed at each of the 4 Decisive Customer Moments, you must continually build Customer Preference.

PREFERENCE GIVES YOU ADVANTAGE

The first thing to understand about preference is that it is not loyalty. Loyalty is steadfast devotion. Loyalty is an unquestioning commitment. Loyalty is being attached—often permanently attached—to an ideal, belief, person, brand, or business. Loyalty is almost extinct in our current business climate.

Preference is about choosing one option over another option or over numerous options because of the valuable benefits the customer receives from one seller during the purchase progression. Preference is not indiscriminate. Preference is not a random choice.

*Preference, in the context of business, is
deliberately making a choice to obtain a real
or perceived benefit—a benefit the customer
values enough to let it influence the decision
about where and from whom to purchase.*

Creating Customer Preference for a business or brand—
regardless of its size or type—delivers a potent advantage to the
seller:

*Preference creates a realistic opportunity for
your business to be your buyer's 1st choice.*

To be clear, Customer Preference, and even being 1st choice,
does not mean that a buyer will overlook issues critical to her—
such as price or convenience—to do business with a particular
company or to buy a particular brand. It simply means that the
buyer will initially place your firm in her "competitive set"—the
very small group of brands that she favors and from which she
will choose very deliberately. Example: You prefer Heineken, but
if it isn't available, you won't leave the restaurant to find it. You
will consider Sam Adams or Amstel before making a final choice.
Example: You prefer John Deere, but to get a better deal, you will
consider Case or Caterpillar before making a final selection.

Even without the promise of "permanent devotion," most
sellers would jump at the chance to be the preferred choice or,
even better, to be the 1st choice in today's fiercely competitive
marketplace. This advantage does not come with a guarantee that

you will be rich and your brand famous, but Customer Preference will produce the incremental growth in sales you need to grow your business. Think of Customer Preference in terms of the following advantages it offers you and not your competitors:

- The buyer will go a *little* out of his way to buy from your firm.

- The buyer will pay *just a bit* more for your firm's products or services.

- The buyer will *consider* buying from your firm without forcing you to bid every time.

- The buyer will *likely* buy from your firm more frequently.

- The buyer will be *slightly* more tolerant when your firm fouls up.

Individually, these benefits may not make or break your business, but collectively they will be the difference between your growth and your decline. Many robust brands and businesses disappear because customers no longer preferred them. This valuable favored position is easily lost, and once lost is hard to regain. Examples are all too numerous:

- Dell is trying to regain the abundant preference it once enjoyed when it was a young, hungry brand with a new idea that others copied.

- Starbucks is trying to rediscover its coffee stardom in the now crowded quality coffee segment it invented.

- Gap lost its Customer Preference to copycats and is now trying to recapture its position as the go-to store for inexpensive, cool clothing.

- Harley-Davidson is struggling to hang on to its king-of-the-road position against aggressive, less expensive imported brands.

- Circuit City never generated Customer Preference because low prices alone don't generate preference (and now Circuit City no longer exists as a brick-and-mortar store, proving that you can't survive without preference).

- Pontiac could not regain the traction it had, because it couldn't decide what segment it was in, and now it is automotive history.

- Converse, once *the* basketball shoe of choice, couldn't retain its narrow slice of the athletic shoe market that global leaders like Nike, Adidas, and Reebok invaded.

To understand preference, you must know that it is highly individual and personal. Each buyer's purchase decision begins with an individual assessment of the numerous choices available in almost every category of business. The buyer sorts through the many choices and decides where to buy based on the tangible and emotional benefits received and on personal preference. This final decision can be captured in a statement like the following:

> *"My preference is based on how good you are*
> *at meeting my wants, needs, and aspirations*
> *and reducing my apprehensions, concerns,*
> *and fears. I have a lot of choices, and I will*
> *decide where to buy after looking at all my*

*options. Given all my options and all the factors
in my purchase decision, I prefer you."*

Customer Preference must be created throughout the purchase progression because the buyer's assessment occurs every time you are in contact with your customer—at each of the 4 Decisive Customer Moments.

Understanding that *preference is the buyer's perception of preference, not the seller's* is an essential first step in regaining some measure of advantage in the transposed buyer-seller equation. In this context, it is not uncommon to hear people say, "That's just my preference." In the language of our self-centered, me-oriented society, this simply means, "I'm special, and my special needs are what count." Why is this puffy "me" stuff so important to an experienced seller like you? Because you, like all sellers, are self-centered too—you say, "I want my business to be the 1st choice over all my competitors." All of us act on our self-interest whether we are buying or selling, and why shouldn't we?

So how do you deliver an experience that makes your customers feel that their needs are what counts? You begin by creating a valuable customer benefit.

Creating Preference with Customer Benefits

We all use the word "benefit" quite a lot, and we know what it means. But what is a "customer benefit"?

*A customer benefit is something that is useful,
helpful, or desirable—a wanted service, a*

43

*product attribute, or a purchasing experience
that you, the buyer, consider advantageous
from your personal perspective.*

*When there is no immediate benefit, there
is no Customer Preference for the seller.*

Sellers do not have to be bigger or even have a better product than their competition to create preference. However, they do have to deliver a benefit that's different from the competition's, and they have to do it at each of the 4 Decisive Moments. Although size and excellence are valuable attributes, you can create a differentiated benefit without them. A strong benefit is usually not expensive to create and maintain, because imagination is free and hard work is the fundamental element of success in every commercial enterprise.

Remember that *a benefit is something a buyer considers advantageous from her personal perspective.* This means that a customer benefit does not have to be monetarily valuable, but of course, it can be. My company earned a quantity discount from FedEx. Although this benefit was monetarily valuable, our firm stayed with this vendor because of its consistent on-time performance, not because of the corporate discount. A Greek restaurant I frequent consistently provides its customers with a complimentary Greek dessert after dinner—it is not monetarily valuable, but it's a tasty benefit that keeps me going back to this restaurant rather than others.

To create preference, sellers do not have to sell a better promise than competitors sell; they must own a better benefit to promise. It is easy for companies to make empty promises. Today's advertising is loaded with promises that sound like "seller think" and "seller talk." However, we buyers live in the world of reality. We know that a promise is intangible and that a benefit is real and substantive. Your buyers can smell the divergence between a lofty promise and a substantive benefit.

A different benefit that is substantive, not hype, will create Customer Preference for your brand or business and make it 1st choice with your buyers.

Sellers do not have to build their brand to create preference; they have to build the benefit their brand stands for. After all, a brand is just a name for a product, service, or company. A brand like BMW is not valuable unless the seller makes it valuable. That is why today's wasteful "brand building" paradigm is both unnecessary and anachronistic. You make your brand valuable to buyers when you explain how your brand will satisfy their wants, needs, and aspirations or reduce their apprehensions, concerns, and fears. You make your brand valuable when you constantly enhance and consistently communicate the primary customer benefit your brand stands for and then firmly attach, cement, or link that benefit to your brand. It is then and only then that your brand becomes valuable to customers and potential customers alike.

A customer benefit cannot be some illusive pledge or deceptive offer or public relations spin. It cannot be something that the customer considers trivial. Most of all, the seller must consistently deliver the customer benefit the seller promised or the buyer will never return. It is even likely that the buyer will trash the seller when sharing buying "horror stories" on Facebook or Twitter or over the fence with a neighbor.

Consistency is an exceptional benefit that few companies today provide, but it can also become so expected that customers often forget how valuable it is. To avoid this you can respectfully remind customers about your consistent performance at some relevant point in your working relationship: "George, I'm proud to report that we had 97 percent defect-free performance for you last year."

To illustrate the importance of consistency, here's a horror story about the danger of not delivering the identical customer benefit off-line and online. It's a situation that occurs all too often in B2B and B2C commerce, and whether it is intentional or unintentional, the seller's reputation will suffer when the inconsistency is discovered.

I was working in my home office while my wife was chatting with a friend in the next room. She was telling her friend about a "shopping victory"—her term for a purchase at a very favorable price. In this instance, she had purchased summer apparel at a 30 percent discount from a well-known chain store's website. When my wife's friend heard this, she was outraged. It seems that she had purchased the identical merchandise from the same chain at one of its retail stores; not being aware of the 30 percent online discount, she had paid full retail price.

This was a failure to deliver consistency at the Make-or-Break Moment of transaction. Within minutes, my wife's friend was off to the store to demand her 30 percent discount. I do not know the outcome, but I do know that this seller was blamed by both my wife and her friend for not delivering the same customer benefit in-store that was being offered online. It's possible that the retailer saved the day at the Keep-or-Lose Moment by admitting its mistake and immediately giving the woman her 30 percent discount. But the result of this type of seller behavior is always the same—the inverse of Customer Preference.

To make your business 1st choice you must understand that your buyer will prefer to buy from you if and only if you consistently deliver the benefit (or benefits) she is seeking at each of the 4 Decisive Customer Moments.

Beyond Benefits: More Ways to Create Customer Preference

In this world where the buyer no longer cares where he buys, creating Customer Preference is not only your best solution—it is your only solution, because buyers are firmly in control of their purchase progression. In resounding corroboration of this argument, a recent article in *Financial Times* about the luxury hotel industry stated: "Never has there been a time when the customer is more in control. Numerous hoteliers talk about the deal-making that direct bookings now entail . . . And because of the transparency of hotel pricing on the [I]nternet, tour operators need to match the last-minute discounting" (Sophy Roberts, "Great luxury hotel deals," August 7, 2009). If you ignore the reality of the importance of building Customer Preference, you must realize that one or more of your competitors will not miss this opportunity to create preference, and you will lose your opportunity to make your business 1st choice.

You have a solution—create Customer Preference for your business with a real sense of urgency at each of the 4 Decisive Customer Moments.

Whereas offering a differentiated benefit is a critical and urgent first step in creating preference, you must equally understand the boundless facets of Customer Preference that can make it enduring and profitable.

- Customer Preference often begins with *likability*. We seldom buy from someone we do not like: "I like the sales rep from one of the many heavy equipment movers under consideration and am inclined to give her the order if her price is within a certain range." *Likability is not a substitute for a customer benefit—it is almost useless as a stand-alone characteristic. However, pairing likability with a wanted customer benefit is a difficult combination for competitors to beat.*

- Customer Preference is frequently based on *trust*. Trust is one of the most powerful influences on purchase: "After interviewing several stock brokers, I've concluded they all seem to offer identical services and fee structures. I'm selecting Smith Barney because I sense I can trust the advisor who is going to be assigned to me." *Trust requires time, patience, and sincerity; when you're trying to build trust, don't be in a hurry, don't be obvious, and most certainly, don't be disingenuous.* Trust is dissimilar from likability in one respect: At certain times and in certain categories—such as very expensive purchases or highly complex products—trust alone can win the day. It is all too easy to lose trust at any of the decisive moments. If you fail to treat a referred customer well, you will lose the trust you built in all the previous moments.

- Customer Preference can be based on *a guarantee.* "I decided to purchase my new sound system from Bose because the company gave me ninety days at no cost to test it out in my home." *Simple guarantees are valued, but complex ones—with almost invisible type—are of little value today. A solid guarantee is a form of trust, so, like trust, it can often win the day and do so quite quickly.* If you do not follow through on that guarantee at the Keep-or-Lose Moment, it is a useless promise.

- Customer Preference can be *the ease of navigating a vendor's website,* which we'll discuss in greater detail when exploring the Now-or-Never Moment. Surely you would like your prospects to make the following statement after viewing your site: "In no time, I found out everything I need to know. After I browse all the other sites, I will probably come back to this site because I prefer this company." *A website is a company's single most influential weapon in its Customer Preference arsenal.*

- Customer Preference can simply be the *best option among those immediately available to us.* "I perceive that the gas station on the right corner looks a little cleaner than the one on the left corner. I turn right into that station because I *need* some gas and *want* a clean bathroom." Don't underestimate the value of seemingly small things that create Customer Preference when sellers appear identical—cleanliness, on-time performance, courtesy, personal appearance, and a host of other factors, including one that we see far too infrequently: a welcoming smile.

• Customer Preference can be *a reflection of what a brand says about the buyer.* These emotional triggers can motivate purchase and often trump many benefits: "I feel elegant in this brand," "I feel proud to buy green," " I feel I got a great value," "I feel like a valued and respected customer," "I feel good about what the brand says about me." These Customer Preferences are simply invaluable.

Customer Preference Will Grow Your Business

Five simple statements capture the power of Customer Preference for businesses today:

*You can create Customer Preference
with big ideas and small ones.*

*You can create Customer Preference
for any size or type of company.*

*You can create Customer Preference to make
your business 1st choice with little if any
investment in infrastructure or advertising.*

Growth generated by Customer Preference is profitable growth because it requires minimal investment.

Building Customer Preference at each of the 4 Decisive Customer Moments will increase your chance of being 1st choice.

Customer Preference will not create loyalty in a world of empowered buyers, nor will it cause customers to line up outside your door. However, Customer Preference will produce profitable incremental sales for your business. Additionally, Customer Preference will continue to generate sales for your business because customers who prefer you are likely to stick with you; they can be motivated to refer your firm to their business contacts, friends, family, and coworkers—creating success during those challenging Keep-or-Lose Moments and Multiplier Moments.

In contrast to the sad stories at the beginning of the chapter, a great many brands and businesses—small and big—endure and thrive because they are the 1st choice of buyers. These firms are determined to retain and enhance Customer Preference because it pays off for them. Consequently, we know many of the famous brands that remain famous because they have created and protected their invaluable reservoir of Customer Preference:

- Apple creates Customer Preference by inspiring its customers to be a part of the elite and passionate community of Apple lovers who feel personally defined by this brand.

- Tiffany creates Customer Preference by placing its merchandise in the most famous box in the world—a familiar robin's-egg blue box that immediately transforms the item, no matter how ordinary or inexpensive, into an immensely valuable and desirable gift.

- Amazon.com creates Customer Preference by making books, and now a great many other items, cheap and easy to buy, gift, ship, and pay for without ever leaving your seat.

- American Airlines creates Customer Preference by enabling flyers and their families to go to destinations they could never otherwise afford by keeping those flyers glued to their original frequent-flyer program.

- FedEx creates Customer Preference by giving shippers peace of mind that their package will arrive on schedule, with the help of an easy-to-use online tracking system.

- Wal-Mart creates Customer Preference by giving shoppers confidence that they will buy good products at low everyday prices.

- Google creates Customer Preference by connecting users in imaginative ways.

Customer Preference also pays off for many giant firms that manufacture and market industrial products and services around the world. These highly successful B2B brands, such as MANN, ABB, 3M, Raytheon, and WellPoint, may not be as well known as some consumer brands, but a B2B that creates Customer Preference for its business reaps the same valuable financial rewards as a consumer business that creates Customer Preference.

Numerous restaurants, merchants, and vendors of all sizes and types create Customer Preference where you live, work, and play. Although you are not loyal to them, you *prefer* to buy from them. Those that retain your *preference* do so in many ways, not just one way, and continue to do so for many years, not just one day.

Here are just a few ways that these local firms create Customer Preference by surprising us, amusing us, reassuring us, helping us, and meeting our "me" wants, needs, and aspirations while reducing our "me" apprehensions, concerns, and fears:

- The nearby storefront restaurant offers us a complimentary beverage if we're kept waiting for a table in their small facility.

- The watch repair service sends a courtesy email to remind us that our watch is ready to be picked up.

- The caulking product comes with a special applicator that lets us get into small crevices and keeps the excess goo from spilling over the tile.

- The plumber leaves during the fourth quarter of an NFL play off game on TV to come over in a snowstorm to fix our kitchen sink that's overflowing.

- The supplier of electrical parts for construction projects gives us same-day delivery for items that are critical to our building timetable.

- The hospital assigns a caring health care professional to inquire about our recovery from outpatient surgery.

The success and business growth that these companies have achieved or are striving for depend on their ability to create *enduring* Customer Preference throughout each of the 4 Decisive Customer Moments.

Enduring Customer Preference (and Profitable Growth) Is Attainable

What follows is a brilliant example of profitable business growth from Customer Preference and a dedication to enduring Customer Preference.

Italy's Fiat Auto makes and markets the legendary Fiat, Alfa Romeo, and Lancia brands in Europe and South America and will soon bring its products to the United States. In 2007, the company revitalized its reputation among customers, dealers, investors, and journalists throughout its European and Latin American markets. In 2008, Fiat Auto announced trading profit of €691 million. *This was an amazing feat because, just three years earlier, Fiat Auto had reported record financial losses.*

The turnaround was engineered by Sergio Marchionne, who was appointed Fiat Auto's CEO in late 2005, the year of the company's financial disaster. Marchionne, who had no automobile experience, promptly secured a favorable agreement to terminate Fiat's joint venture agreement with General Motors, which had an urgent need for capital. To substantially reduce his overhead and build an entirely new Fiat Auto, Marchionne then removed an entire floor of old-line executives.

His next step was to find someone to develop and lead a strategy that would transform the company's products and marketing. He chose thirty-nine-year-old Luca De Meo. In October 2007, Luca told me that he and two others developed the strategy to transform Fiat's Customer Preference. They accomplished this seemingly insurmountable task in just one week. When I asked Luca how they accomplished this feat in such a short time, he replied, "We had no choice; we were bleeding."

Luca called his one-page preference-building strategy the "Five S's" and described each "S" in such brief, plain language that its brilliance might be overlooked. He graciously agreed to let me share that strategy here.

The Fiat Five S's: A Preference-Building Strategy

1. **Surprise:** Fiat will be a *conquest* brand—our products will be *different* from competitive brands.

2. **Speed:** Fiat will be *fast to market* our product development time will be cut in half and remain foreshortened—and our cars will respond to the European and South American customers' desire for speed on the open road.

3. **Simplicity:** The Fiat language will be *simplicity*—Fiat's products will be simple to operate, and our ways of working will be simple, not bureaucratic or complex.

4. **Smile.** Fiat will be the *smiling* brand—our customers will view our products as fresh and contemporary, not old and institutional.

5. **Style:** Fiat will be #1 in *style*—style is our Italian cultural asset and our company heritage.

I asked Luca how long it took to get approval for the *deceptively simple* "Five Ss" strategy. He said, "We met with Marchionne for an hour and walked out with his approval because we were all determined to be on a *fast* track."

To create Customer Preference for the Fiat brand, Fiat introduced a series of new models, all designed with modern, *simple* features. The Fiat 500 (*Cinquecento*)—a spectacular new compact car—would be the firm's *conquest* brand. Fiat launched the cool 500 in a wide variety of stylish and outrageous interior and exterior color schemes on July 4, 2007, the second anniversary of the firm's incredible rags-to-riches story.

The anticipation of and expectation for Fiat's new car did not rely on traditional media—it began early and focused on the Internet and public relations to *create preference* at the Now-or-Never Moment among influential young drivers. The results of this early digital effort were remarkable and heavily publicized.

The international press also witnessed the *surprising* launch festivities that took place in Turin, home of Fiat's global headquarters. To generate even more excitement and drama for the Fiat 500 introduction and to expand the Now-or-Never Moment, people all over the world were able to view the launch thanks to online streaming video of the "500 Wants You" celebration.

Fiat transformed Turin's Po River into a promenade for colorful, sensational, and sometimes outrageous events. Barges, acrobats, water-skiers, fireworks, brilliantly lit fountains, and huge fiery candles preceded the sixty performers who, in an extraordinary aerial choreography, lifted a gigantic model of the 500 into the illuminated sky to create *smiles* for the new Fiat 500.

Then, to assure that prospects could view the brand's *style* and variety up close, five hundred colorful Fiat 500 automobiles crossed the Po and continued through the winding streets of the ancient and aristocratic city of Turin (and later through other European cities). Fiat was reborn as a *conquest* brand.

The *surprises* didn't stop with purely commercial events. The Fiat 500 sponsored a national fund-raising drive to help the more than fifty-five hundred babies born prematurely in Italy every year. Luca explained the charity initiative as "an effort on behalf of a little car with a big heart to transmit joy and hope." He added, "Our company must play a meaningful role in ecology, safety, and transportation for the disabled." Luca believes that "values add value," a sure way to build preference at each of the 4 Decisive Customer Moments.

Fiat established Customer Preference for its brand, models, dealers, and prospects by changing the way the company thought and acted:

- Fiat swept out the deadwood rather than layering its new organizational model on the old Fiat bureaucratic foundation.

- Fiat established exceptionally high new quality standards.

- Fiat reduced its timetable for product to market.

- Fiat gave determined talent the authority to be brave, bold, and creative.

- Fiat restructured its dealer organization—aggressive new dealers replaced dealers who were not performing.

- Fiat consistently communicated with all its audiences—used public relations creatively, employed imaginative events, and made full use of interactive media at every first point of contact—to succeed at the Now-or-Never Moment.

Luca concluded his amazing turnaround story by emphasizing that the company was committed to creating *enduring* Customer Preference for its brands and products. Here are just a few current examples of this continuing commitment to Customer Preference—all designed to link Fiat with *surprise, smile,* and *style*:

- Fiat's website allows prospective buyers to build a customized 500 by choosing from a vast array of options. Go to www.fiat.co.uk and smile as you configure your personalized 500.

- Fiat and MTV sponsored the 500 PICNIC, a fun, music-filled event held in sixteen cities around the world. A special jury reviewed amateur videos submitted via a dedicated website and selected the performing artists.

- Fiat and Microsoft developed a new application that teaches customers to drive greener, consume less fuel, and cut CO_2 emissions.

- Fiat sponsored a "Fiat 500 Wants a Mascot" contest. A committee of the "500 Wants You" community selected Dante, a "small, strong, curious character, just like the 500," in the words of Dante's creator, one of seven hundred entrants.

This is an innovative illustration of enduring Customer Preference on a grand scale. However, enduring Customer Preference is not about scale, quantity, marketing spin, irrelevant antics, or investment in advertising or infrastructure. Enduring Customer Preference just requires a simple strategy—a brief, clear, new way of thinking and working that

- *defines the most substantive customer benefit(s)* the company offers its customers, and

- *links this substantive customer benefit with the company's name or brand* consistently, repetitively, and imaginatively.

Valuable Lessons from Saturn's Failure and Fiat's Success

You can learn valuable lessons from the Saturn tragedy, described in Chapter 2, and the contrasting success of Fiat. *These divergent examples will help you create and sustain Customer Preference at your 4 Decisive Customer Moments.*

Here are the lessons in order of priority:

Strategy—This is the starting place for every enterprise because strategy is the definitive influence on enduring success.

Ironically, the basic flaws in Saturn's strategy were their likable messages—"a new kind of car company" and "rethink everything." Both messages reflected their misguided strategy— they were about the seller, not the buyer. Saturn had developed a car company strategy, not a customer strategy. *Strategy must be customer-centric.* In contrast, Fiat's strategy focused on the customer—*the customer's desire and need for surprise, speed, simplicity—that smiling feeling a customer gets when he thinks of his car, style, and a different car to own and drive.* Saturn had a short-term dedication to Customer Preference; Fiat had a passionate commitment to enduring Customer Preference.

To be successful in today's customer-dominant selling environment, you must adopt a new customer-centric strategy for your business.

Structure—A company's way of thinking and working has a profound influence on the company's ability to design and implement a strategy that creates enduring success.

Saturn, the "new kind of car company," was born as a layer on top of an old business model—a rigid, bloated bureaucratic GM structure that had at its core a way of thinking and acting that was slow, inefficient, and locked in the past. That same criticism has been leveled against Detroit carmaker Chrysler. According to Financialtimes.com/Companies/Automobiles, streamlining management and processes alike is "'going to be job number one [for Sergio Marchionne and his team at Fiat] at Chrysler: dealing with the bloated control structure,' says Stuart Pearson, autos analyst with Credit Suisse in London" (Bernard Simon and John Reed, "Italians Get to Work at Chrysler," September 3, 2009).

Saturn was not encouraged to think in the long term, was not able to confront problems with a sense of urgency, and was not mandated to take aggressive action. The seven-year inception-to-market period invited tough competition, and the lack of readiness to introduce winning new models soon after launch prevented Saturn from sustaining Customer Preference. Contrast this tragedy with Fiat's clean break with its bureaucratic heritage; immediate transformation into a nimble, entrepreneurial-like operating model; and firm dedication to enduring Customer Preference.

To be successful in today's highly competitive global marketplace, you must function within a structure that encourages a long-term strategic

*vision, facilitates immediate confrontation of
obstacles, and mandates sound decision making,
creative solutions, and aggressive action.*

Imagination—The element that is lacking in most businesses, regardless of size or type, is imagination.

Saturn was, in reality, a new kind of car company at the beginning—the concept and marketing were imaginative at the launch. Saturn's advertising and public relations were dramatically different from the prevailing "car think" and "car talk." However, Saturn did not "rethink everything"—it did not think about its after-launch future. Saturn's imagination just stopped soon after the brand's introduction.

Fiat continues to innovate, especially in the two most vital areas of its business—the imaginative design of its products and the imaginative use of digital communications, social media, and public relations that engages and empowers its customers, dealers, suppliers, and the press and transforms them into an enthusiastic Fiat community. Fiat is also engaging its community by its early use of codesign, using digital technology that allows customers to personalize aspects of the Fiat 500 online.

This use of codesign technology is in its infancy, but I believe that very soon almost every site in the world will encourage and enable customers to codesign—a process that will ignite the imagination of the buyer and the seller alike while cementing Customer Preference for the seller. Tomorrow is not here yet, so I cannot confirm that Fiat's success will endure. But judging by my lengthy meeting with the Fiat automotive management team, it is a good bet that Fiat will sustain its imagination and Customer Preference.

A sound strategy and an effective structure are simply not enough—imagination must start in the corner office and radiate out into every corner of the business. Imagination is not an idea or a stream of ideas—imagination is the originality of thinking and acting that makes a business different. Lack of financial resources is a lame excuse, because imagination is free.

The Need for a New Business Model

There is no such thing as a universal business model—every category, every business, every competitive set, and every locale in the world requires a business model tailored to the customer's individual wants, needs, and aspirations and her apprehensions, concerns, and fears.

There is no such thing as a permanent business model—the changes in global commerce and politics, the fluctuations of the local and global economies, the introduction of new technologies, the evolving management structures and revolving door of corporate power, and the ever-shifting human equation all require a flexible and evolving model that is sensitive to these fluctuating customer influences. GM's trial run of a joint venture with eBay to sell cars online in late 2009 underscores the way a company must try to change as market conditions change.

Although it is unrealistic to expect any business model to be universal or permanent, there is an *urgent need for a new global business model that is consistent with three realities:*

Reality #1: Today's buyer is in control of the purchase progression.

Reality #2: Today's buyer is intensely self-serving.

Reality #3: Today's buyer no longer cares where she buys.

Your new business model must be customer-centric—it must make this a new way of thinking and working a reality. Here is what you and all sellers must do to make your customer-centric business model work:

- Today's sellers must change and learn how to make their firms 1st choice.

- Today's sellers must "live" Customer Preference by learning how to focus all their financial and human resources on the creation of enduring Customer Preference.

- Today's sellers must create repeat customers and advocates by learning how to transform prospects into customers and customers into endorsers.

- Today's sellers must create "communities" for their companies or brands by optimizing websites and employing digital communications, social media, and public relations to engage and involve their tribe in their company's success.

- Today's sellers must use training as a differentiating strategic asset by teaching all those in contact with prospects and customers to think like buyers think.

- Today's sellers must employ metrics to measure Customer Preference and conversion at every stage of the purchase progression.

In the chapters that follow, you will discover how your new customer-centric business model will influence your success at each of your 4 Decisive Customer Moments. You will also find out why Customer Preference requires little or no investment in infrastructure or advertising. Each chapter contains numerous examples and provides illustrations of Customer Preference in businesses of every size and type.

Make no mistake—you simply cannot get by with just

- a friendly smile at your brief Now-or-Never Moment,

- a warm handshake at your Make-or-Break Moment,

- a form letter with a satisfaction survey at your Keep-or-Lose Moment, and

- a "come back and see us" mailer at your invaluable Multiplier Moment.

Your Now-or-Never Moment is next up.

Take a Moment to Consider...

whether your business is creating enduring Customer Preference.

1. Is your business customer-centric?

2. Does your business deliver a benefit that your customer values and that will differentiate your firm from your competitors?

3. Is your business acting and communicating in a manner that will encourage the prospective customer to like, trust, and respect your firm and staff?

If you are not confident that your company can create Customer Preference at each of the 4 Decisive Customer Moments, you must remedy the problems or you won't be able to grow your business.

4

NOW-OR-NEVER—
YOUR FIRST BRIEF CONTACT

Is your firm ready to capture your prospects right now?

Imagine that a potential customer has contacted your business for the very first time. This person is in touch with you because he has already searched for your product or service online, is very knowledgeable about it, knows the range of prices in the marketplace, and is *now actively seeking what you are selling.*

This prospect intends to buy from you or one of your hungry competitors; however, he is approaching you with wants, needs, and aspirations and with apprehensions, concerns, and fears.

Now imagine your company's response to this first contact. How will you provide far more than the product and service this prospect is seeking? How will you deliver the help, advice, and performance this individual requires and expects at his first point of contact with your firm? Visualize how you will create Customer Preference at your Now-or-Never Moment.

Does the scenario you imagine give you confidence that your business is ready for your fleeting, critically important Now-or-Never Moment?

Your Now-or-Never Moment is gone forever
if you do not grab it immediately!

If you are not yet sure that you can create Customer Preference for your business when a prospect contacts you for the first time, you are not alone—you are in the same situation as far too many other business leaders whose historic way of thinking and selling was only effective when sellers were in control. Yesterday's compliant, naïve, loyal buyers no longer exist.

Creating Customer Preference is a very effective strategy, but like all ambitious strategies, it will not work unless it is an integral part of the seller's customer-centric strategy. The usual cause of failure is lack of discipline and creativity. You can significantly increase the probability of converting a prospect into a customer by preparing yourself and every part of your organization to generate Customer Preference at your fragile first encounter with a prospect.

No one would doubt that first encounters take place every minute of every day all over the world, and I am sure you agree that they take place quite often in your business. Given this reality, not anticipating and preparing for this decisive moment is counterproductive. If you bungle this encounter with your prospect, you fail to gain a valuable customer, an enduring customer relationship, and a brand advocate, and you lose one incremental sale after another. But you actually lose a great deal more if this prospect is not persuaded to move forward with you—you also lose some part of your investment in

- customer generation,
- every person on your staff,
- every piece of equipment you own,
- every store in your chain, and
- every product in your inventory.

You have made these investments and many others to generate profitable growth; however, your business will never achieve this goal if your business has low prospect-to-customer conversion ratios at your Now-or-Never Moment.

If you are not consistently converting prospects into customers at their first point of contact with your firm, your investments will be wasted and your competitors will win the new customers you seek.

What you lose when you do not win at your Now-or-Never Moment underscores your need to throw out your obsolete selling model and reinforces your need to adopt a new customer-centric business model.

The first step, as always, is to think like a buyer.

What's Going On in the Customer's Head at Your Now-or-Never Moment?

To learn to think like a buyer thinks, *pretend that you are the buyer* at some Now-or-Never Moments in seemingly insignificant buying situations.

- You walk into a store to buy a pair of running shoes that you saw in this store's ad in today's newspaper. Two customers are trying on shoes with the help of salespeople. While you are browsing the shelves, two other salespeople are chatting away at the back of the store; they do not greet you or offer to help you. *What do you do in this situation?*

- You call a plumbing supply firm that another contractor recommended. Someone answers, but she asks you to hold while she finishes another call. You remain on hold for what seems like a lifetime. *What do you do in this situation?*

- You are searching for a particular technology product on a seller's website. You see a lot of products but not the one you need. You use the site's question prompt to ask whether the seller can special order your product. Two days pass without a response. *What do you do in this situation?*

What you do in each of these situations is, of course, *go elsewhere to buy what you need.*

When today's buyer makes contact with you, it is an important and unambiguous signal that this buyer is ready to buy from someone. *Why else would this prospect be prospecting?*

Here is what your prospect is thinking: *I've done my homework. I have a lot of choices, and I'll decide where to buy after looking at all my options. This is your moment to persuade me to buy from you.*

Here is what you should be thinking: *My prospect is ready to buy and therefore will be susceptible to my persuasive Customer Preference.*

This is your Now-or-Never Moment, and you must have a customer-centric business model to ensure that you capture this ready-to-buy prospect. Otherwise, this valuable buyer will slip into the hands of a competitor.

Where Are Most of Your Prospects Coming From?

First contacts can originate from a wide variety of sources. Knowing the source of your contact can be a valuable customer-centric data point because it reveals how this customer thinks and buys, and this insight will help you capture this prospect for your firm.

Your initial contact from a potential buyer can be intentional or unintentional on the prospect's part. It would be valuable for you to know what motivated this prospect to contact you and how she chose to contact you, because it will help you establish a relationship with her and search for more prospects just like her.

Much of the time, a prospect will proudly volunteer this information: "Betty Smith loves your shop—she thought I might like it too because we share the same tastes and values." Or, "My drill bit manufacturer has gone out of business, and I hear that you guys have some new technology that will give us more durable bits than we've been using." But if the prospect does not volunteer this information, you can ask for it in a brief, gentle way: "Would you mind telling me why you decided to contact our firm about your recruiting requirements?" If this does not work, quickly move on to another topic of interest to the prospect.

Later in your conversation, the person might reveal this information unintentionally: "Your site described your special techniques for remodeling kitchens—could you tell me more about this way of working please?" Bingo—she has been on your website!

This goes beyond simply gathering the information. Establishing metrics that will accurately measure and compare the quantity of contacts that originate from each of your sources will enable you to concentrate on those sources that are most important to your business and improve your contact generation from other sources. If you do not already know the sources of most of your prospects, waste no time in establishing a system of metrics.

Here are the seven most likely origins of contact for most industries and businesses:

- Website
- Word of mouth
- Email or phone
- Social media
- Chance encounter
- Advertising
- Trade journal content

Obviously, sources of first contacts vary from industry to industry and from company to company, so there is no uniform order of importance, with two exceptions—website and word of mouth. Social media may very soon replace or merge with these origins of contacts, but for now, your website and word-of-mouth marketing are your two most important weapons in your arsenal for engaging customers, particularly profitable ones.

Your Biggest Opportunity and Vulnerability Is Your Website

Your site is likely to be the most meaningful source of first encounters with your firm. Every day your firm's site becomes more important to the success of your enterprise, regardless of its size or type, because more and more people are using technology in their buying regimen.

Your critical Now-or-Never Moment can be seller-positive if your site captures the buyer in the first few seconds after the buyer clicks on. When the seller's home page does its work, it is the seller's biggest opportunity to transform a prospect into a customer, because all eight hundred pounds of this eight-hundred-pound gorilla are working for the seller.

However, this fraction of a moment after the buyer clicks on the seller's site can also be seller-negative—the seller's single most vulnerable instant. If the seller's home page does not capture the buyer in the first few seconds after the buyer clicks on, there is absolutely no opportunity for recovery because all eight hundred pounds of the gorilla are sitting on the buyer's finger as the buyer clicks away. At that click, you are out of consideration.

*How many times a day is your site eliminating
your firm from further consideration?*

Please go to the Amazon.com site. Take a close look at Amazon's home page. See how inviting the large, clean, white space is and how easily and quickly you can search for what you are seeking. Amazon's site navigation is a valuable customer benefit. You cannot miss the big picture of the latest item: the Amazon Kindle, the new way to read almost anything anywhere, or the tempting seasonal offerings. Moreover, you will see "Your Recent History" and these simply worded offers of assistance: "Where's My Stuff?" and "Need Help?" These useful phrases are also valuable customer benefits.

Amazon's site provides customers a huge benefit because its design is exceptionally efficient. All too often a seller's home page is cluttered with words and pictures irrelevant to the buyer's primary reason for clicking on its site.

*Most home pages do not clearly define the single most
important customer benefit the seller is offering, so the
buyer's finger instantly clicks the seller into oblivion.*

Now look at your competitors' sites and your own site. If your site does not stand up to comparative scrutiny, it is likely that you are losing most if not all of your first contacts at your Now-or-Never Moments.

The visitor to your site is in total control of his purchase progression with your firm. Your home page must convince your prospects that you will deliver what they want and must address their emotional needs and concerns. Therefore, *your site must do four things extraordinarily well:*

- Engage the visitor instantly.
- Enable the visitor to quickly find what he came to the site for.
- Immediately and clearly communicate your firm's primary customer benefit.
- Instantly create Customer Preference by demonstrating how you will perform for him; how you will provide consistent service after the sale; how you have met or exceeded the expectations of other customers; how you will fulfill his wants, needs, and aspirations and allay his apprehensions, concerns, and fears.

Your site must be customer-centric—it is the buyer's window into your company, not a soapbox from which your company pounds its chest. Your site is the center of your buyer's "me" universe because navigating a site is a highly personal experience— a one-on-one contact between the prospect and you. Your site must create customer persuasion.

Claire Cain Miller, technology and business reporter for the *New York Times*, addresses another issue that you cannot afford to overlook—any flaws in the design of your website or glitches in the technology that could prevent you from closing an online sale. "Shoppers spent $130 billion online in the last year . . . [but companies] missed out on billions more because customers abandoned their carts once they ran into problems while checking out" ("Closing the Deal at the Virtual Checkout Counter," *New York Times*, October 11, 2009).

Want to see a site that gets it all right? Go to 1-800-Flowers. com. The company's online sales of flowers and gift baskets were about $700 million in 2009, and it has used analytics software to manage its site for years, keeping it updated with new prices, new options, new deals—often hourly. The company also uses mobile applications to make it easier for customers to purchase from their cell phones. And "in the last six months [of 2009]... 1-800-Flowers.com has improved the conversion rate—browsers to buyers—on its Web site by 20 percent with more finely targeted pages and e-mail promotions" (Steve Lohr, "A Data Explosion Remakes Retailing," *New York Times*, January 3, 2010). And it takes only an instant to see why the company's conversion rate is on the rise:

- Its site engages you instantly with photos of beautiful bouquets on the main page and compelling taglines (such as "Most popular gifts for every occasion" and "Bestsellers starting at $24.99"). Those bouquets are updated frequently to meet the needs and demands of buyers.

- You can immediately purchase any of the featured bouquets (prices are displayed beneath) or you can go into one of the featured collections. When I looked, the options were Birthday, Same-Day Delivery, Gifts Under $30, Roses, Sympathy, and Just Because—collections that meet the needs of most buyers on most days.

- Most bouquets are offered in different sizes, allowing you to get the bouquet you want at the price you want. And you can see images of the bouquets in different sizes, so you don't have to guess what your bouquet will look like.

- Below the images of the bouquets, there is a highlighted "special mobile offers" section that allows visitors to type in their cell phone numbers and see what special offers they're eligible for.

- And if you are on the main page for very long without clicking through, a chat window pops up offering online help from a representative in selecting "the perfect gift."

Few business leaders want to believe or acknowledge that their site is not performing for them. But few put the time, energy, and investment into making their site as successful as 1-800-Flowers.com.

Most sellers' sites are dictated by the firm's leader or directed by well-meaning employees, competent external techs, or graphic designers—all dedicated to the task, but frequently using trite seller language. Your site has to show that you think like your buyer, so I urge that you appoint someone who thinks like a buyer does to direct and manage the technology and design. This is worth repeating—your site must capture your prospect immediately, enable the visitor to discover what he wants to discover, and facilitate purchase.

There is no better business investment than a well-designed, well-functioning, customer-centric website—it can make your business 1st choice at the first point of contact.

The challenge of creating a compelling online presence does not only relate to capturing online buyers. Sellers can *forget*

about the distinction between online and off-line buyers—there is none.
Today's off-line buyer, much like today's online buyer, spends a
lot of time looking at options online. In the context of online
evaluation of potential places to buy, *all buyers* are now determined to

- be knowledgeable about the products and services they seek;
- consider multiple seller options;
- purchase when, how, and from whom they choose;
- select the seller that delivers the most benefits; and
- remain independent.

*All buyers now enjoy the independence they
have gained from shopping online before
purchasing either online or off-line.*

My perspective of today's radically changed buyer is consistent with the views of Andy Mulholland, global chief technology
officer of the Capgemini Group, and Nick Earle, vice president
for Cisco Services, European Markets, who coauthored a new,
informative book entitled *Mesh Collaboration*: "Digital literacy
can be assumed, and it can also be assumed that people have the
systems at home to be able to do things and behave differently
than they have in the past." Note that the authors said "people,"
not "online buyers." Online and off-line buyers are one and the
same in the context of their shared determination to use technology to be knowledgeable, selective, well prepared, and most
of all, *independent.*

Recently I shopped online for a unique toy for my young grandson's birthday. I chose the FAO Schwarz site because this toy seller has a reputation for unusual items for kids. On the site's home page, I found numerous toys, but they were far from unusual—they were ordinary. I was disappointed, and started to click off. Luckily, I saw the toolbar that highlighted gift items with a difference—"Science," "Books," "Games," "Creativity." That encouraged me to think I might have come to the right site after all, so I hung in.

Before trolling for the special toy I was searching for, I found a blurb all the way at the bottom of the home page that described the firm's "one-year satisfaction guarantee." This was an influential but hidden customer benefit—after all, I was a toy buyer worried that his grandson would not like the toy or that he already had one like it.

On the FAO Schwarz home page, I also found an obscure listing among many other small listings: "History." When I clicked this link, I found other customer benefits such as "145-year tradition for unique and exclusive offerings from around the world" and "concern about children's health and safety." This was far more than "history"—it was buried Customer Persuasion.

Although I had to work far too hard to be persuaded to buy, I finally purchased a cool learning game online, with the confidence that I could return it to FAO Schwarz if necessary. It wasn't necessary—my grandson loved it and I was relieved.

Other buyers may not be this patient. So take another very close look at your site and ask yourself these two paramount questions:

*Does your home page instantly
create Customer Preference?*

*Does your site make buying easy
and quick for your customer?*

If your answer is "no" to either of these questions, take prompt action to reconstruct, redesign, or both reconstruct and redesign your website, and remember to put someone who thinks like a buyer in charge of this vitally important mission.

*To generate incremental growth, you cannot
afford to lose a single customer because you
failed to create persuasion at your Now-or-
Never Moment when she clicked on your site.*

Here is just one of the thousands of first contacts that happen every second of every day on the Internet:

I know a vice president of purchasing at a large manufacturer of pharmaceutical products. She was tasked with the job of finding a packaging supplier for a new line of liquid vitamin supplements. Her CEO wanted a distinctive container that would stand out on the shelf and enable customers to easily and accurately control dosage. The purchasing executive and her staff studied the sites of fifty-plus suppliers from around the world; the group was blown away by the work of a small packaging firm in Japan.

The Japanese site featured packages that were exceptionally well designed and highly functional. The purchasing agent made contact via email and promptly received a proposal. The proposed design fulfilled the specifications of the pharmaceutical firm as well as the expectations of the purchasing team, but the price quote was far higher than the price range in the firm's request for proposal (RFP). Rather than move on to other suppliers, the purchasing team decided to work closely with the Japanese firm to bring down the cost without compromising quality.

This is a vivid example of a site that not only grabbed a prospect—it captured the prospect by creating Customer Preference at the first point of contact. This influential Customer Preference encouraged the buyer to work with the seller through the purchase progression to bring the price down. If the Customer Preference had been less influential—if the seller's website had been only marginally better than a competitor's at engaging the buyer—the buyer might have simply rejected the high-priced proposal and moved on to the next-best option.

Sellers can also take advantage of the ease with which they can track potential customers through their activity on the Web. If, for example, you walk into a jeweler's or an optician's, those proprietors have "no way of knowing who [you are] or how to get [you] back in the store, but online, [companies] can do all that" (Claire Cain Miller, "Closing the Deal at the Virtual Checkout Counter," *New York Times*, October 11, 2009).

Technology is one of the key mandates in your new customer-centric business model as evidenced by this reality: a prospect's email address is the most valuable tool in your marketing tool chest. Create opportunities to secure email addresses at the Now-or-Never Moment.

*You and your entire organization must
learn how to win today's Internet-informed
buyer, who routinely gets smart online before
buying from a supplier or a store off-line.*

Word-of-Mouth Customers Are Profitable Customers

Positive word of mouth is another important source of prospects, because these individuals are "presold" by the person who suggested your firm.

*Word of mouth is the source that is least
expensive at your Now-or-Never Moment.*

Word-of-mouth customers are highly profitable because there are no costs associated with their acquisition. They are also highly valuable because they are likely to spend more freely with someone they know they can trust. Positive word of mouth can be generated by asking a well-satisfied customer to recommend you to his family, friends, and associates; if you've built Customer Preference with this customer, he should enjoy spreading the word about his "find." I'll discuss this more in chapters 6 and 7.

A first encounter from a word-of-mouth source should turn out this way:

My daughter was about to have a milestone birthday, and I volunteered to give her a late-day party at a wine bar near her home. She put me in touch with the proprietor, and I dropped by his place of business to work out the menu of fun finger foods and to select the wine. He made suggestions about the food and wine that enabled me to stay within my budget without skimping on quality. He remained personally involved with every aspect of the party, and it was a huge success.

I became a customer of this wine bar, and we have worked together on quite a few entertaining occasions. I have told some friends and associates about him and the added value he provides customers. When I need a bottle or two of wine, I often trade with a wine store that is closer, but I keep going back to the guy at the wine bar when it is a meaningful occasion for me. That first point of contact with a person and a place that I had never heard of has been a good experience for us both because my daughter had "presold" me and the seller created Customer Preference at my first point of contact.

This brings us to the mass word-of-mouth game-changer—social media. It amplifies word of mouth exponentially—it transforms word of mouth from a person-to-person medium into a mass medium. Through social media, customers become a community of talkers, traders of information and experiences, and most important, listeners. And social media allow sellers to play a heavier role in word-of-mouth marketing by using Facebook and Twitter and by maximizing the effectiveness of other online tools, such as blogs.

Social media not only connect buyers to buyers, they connect sellers to buyers and buyers to sellers. They enable sellers to listen to and learn directly from buyers, virtually eliminating the marketing researcher middleman who has historically been the only authoritative connection between buyers and sellers. Social media can help you interpret your buyers' thoughts, ideas, prejudices, desires, and dreams. Give social media a try before your competition does.

How to Increase Your Odds at First Contact

Most sellers say that "selling" their product or service at the first point of contact is their number one priority. However, in the business trenches where I've lived for the past forty-five years, I have found a more effective agenda for the first point of contact with a prospect: *Your number one priority should be to get your prospect to like you and trust you.* Do not act like an old-style seller who is intensely focused on closing and moving on to the next sale. To achieve the goals of getting your prospect to like and trust you, try the following:

- Dig for useful information about this decision maker *in advance of* the meeting, keeping in mind that you are not the only seller who is trying to get this person to say yes.

- Find out how much time the prospect wants to spend with you—never exceed this time limit unless the prospect asks you to, because this will damage or destroy your chance of success.

- Listen very carefully and often, and watch your prospect's body language, because he will probably reveal valuable information you will not get when you are doing all the talking.

- Ask questions that will help you find out about this prospect's wants, needs, and aspirations and his apprehensions, concerns, and fears that are driving him to buy the product or service you're offering at this time. Prospects will often tell sellers exactly what they want, but too many sellers are too busy talking to learn this invaluable insight.

- Try to ascertain, very subtly, whether the person you are talking to is the decision maker or the gatekeeper—if the answer is gatekeeper, try to convert your contact into an advocate for your firm by providing proof of performance or references the decision maker will respect.

My cousin was looking for a place to buy a modest piece of jewelry for his wife to celebrate their anniversary. He had already shopped online and had some stores and items in mind. He also knew that many items were at the price he wanted to pay. When he described his shopping experience as an "awful ordeal" that nevertheless ended well, I became very interested, because it demonstrated how unprepared most off-line sellers are when confronted with prospects who have done their homework online.

My cousin said that all but one jewelry store, the place where he purchased, ignored or trivialized his Internet research about the merchandise he wanted and the price he wanted to pay. One seller denied that the company's site displayed the item he was interested in, even though it was posted for all to see. Another seller stated that the price range my cousin had seen on various sites was "out of date," and still another insisted on showing him only items that were well out of his price range.

Like most customers who shop off-line but do their homework online, my cousin was well informed and proud of the time and effort he'd spent in preparing for his shopping experience. If any of these sellers had bothered to listen to what he was saying, they would have been able to discern that important factor. That is why it was an "awful ordeal" for him but a great example to share with you. Sellers who are so focused on making the sale and therefore feel that they have to establish themselves as the sole possessor of category knowledge are living in yesterday. These "yesterday sellers"—sellers who refuse to change, who refuse to listen to what the customer is saying and then find a way to fulfill his true needs—will not survive in today's marketplace, which is populated by shrewd online shoppers who want to be treated with respect, not with indifference or disdain.

Preparation and training are key mandates in your customer-centric business model—and they are vital to your ability to capture prospects at your Now-or-Never Moment.

Mistakes Can Happen at First Contact

No matter how hard a seller tries, stuff happens—big stuff and small stuff as well as real stuff and perceived stuff. This stuff can disrupt your efforts to create Customer Preference at the first contact or any of the other Decisive Customer Moments.

Here is what a seller can do about this negative situation at the Now-or-Never Moment: *Anticipate it. Prepare for it. Train for it.*

Anticipate when negative customer reactions are most likely to happen in your business. There is no way to think of everything, of course, but preparing a list of potential problem points is very valuable.

Prepare a list of remedial actions that you can take at each potential problem point you have identified. To supplement those specific actions, here are a few actions you can take when a problem jumps up out of nowhere at a Now-or-Never Moment:

- Act instantly and courteously to isolate the aggrieved person from other customers, to deprive her of an audience.

- Apologize in a manner that is sincere and believable. Do not hesitate to do it again.

- Contrary to popular belief, the customer is not always right, but never let your customer feel that she is not right.

- Do not delay taking control of a potentially explosive situation, and do not jump to conclusions about the truth of the aggrieved person's complaint.

- Immediately reduce the tension by listening to the complaint without interrupting. Ask a question or two in a nonthreatening tone if it will reduce the tension or help you find a solution.

- Explain that you will discuss the situation with the employee involved, but do not state that you will discipline or terminate the person, as that is a matter to be handled later with the employee.

- Offer a meaningful solution and/or some tangible expression of your concern, but never offer an angry prospect something insignificant, as this will surely make the matter worse. Do not let the customer leave without a solution, as this will allow time for the problem to grow out of proportion.

Train everyone involved in any kind of contact with a dissatisfied first-time customer—from the staff member at the initial point of contact to the person who must manage a difficult Now-or-Never Moment.

You cannot just talk about being customer-centric—*you have to be customer-centric by creating and maintaining Customer Preference.* This requires a high standard of performance; rigorous training to assure performance; metrics to measure performance; and prompt, appropriate action when performance falls short of customer expectations.

To achieve consistent success at your Now-or-Never Moment, you must be obsessed with Customer Preference.

When you transform a prospect into a potential customer at your brief Now-or-Never Moment, you will have earned the opportunity to close the sale at your lengthy Make-or-Break Moment, the subject of the next chapter.

Take a Moment to Consider...
*how you can create preference at your **Now-or-Never Moment.***

1. Evaluate the single most potent tool you have to convert prospects into customers—your website. Be sure that your site's design and content are customer-centric and that it's easy and quick to navigate. Your home page must grab the visitor, differentiate you from your competitors, and immediately convey the primary benefit(s) you offer the prospect. To obtain each visitor's email address, encourage your visitors to interact with you, using such tools as "sample us," "sign up for a free estimate," "take a test drive," "free consultation," and the like. Consistently update your site and improve its ability to compel immediate online purchase or additional off-line consideration.

2. Examine the existing data you have on prospect-to-customer conversion at the first brief moment of contact with your firm. If you don't have reliable data, create a system or invest in one, because you must measure conversion, source of contact (site, phone, word of mouth, social media, etc.), and conversion trends at each of the 4 Decisive Customer Moments.

3. Compare the volume of contacts from each source, and determine which sources of contacts offer more potential for the future. Define the actions that can be taken to drive additional contact at your high-priority points of contact. Establish ambitious but achievable goals at each source, and experiment with actions to achieve those goals. Continue to monitor results and test new actions.

4. Train every employee who may be in touch with the prospect at the first point of contact, and continue to evaluate these employees' ability to create Customer Preference and facilitate conversion. Consider implementing a weekly stand-up for the most interesting customer moments and a recognition program for the most successful conversion of the week. Remember how persuasive likability and trust are at first contact. Prepare a list of potential questions from prospects, and keep adding new questions to the list. How well and how promptly questions are answered will determine the level of Customer Preference you create. If you or your staff have live contact with the prospect, remember that listening is more valuable than talking.

As you prepare for your **Now-or-Never Moment,** keep in mind that purchase is a progression and that you must succeed at your prospect's first point of contact.

5

MAKE-OR-BREAK—THE LENGTHY TRANSACTION PROCESS

Is your company consistently converting prospects into buyers? Do you measure your rate of conversion? Are you taking every possible action to optimize your conversion ratio?

The prospect you met for the very first time at your Now-or-Never Moment and converted into a potential customer is now ready to make a purchase. This person has done his homework online, feels empowered, and will buy from you or from a limited selection of competitors who are just as determined to make the sale as you are.

This is your Make-or-Break Moment, because the extended period of consideration, negotiation, and decision to purchase is when far too many transactions fall through. And your ability to turn prospects into customers at the lengthy moment of transaction will make or break your business.

*You must create Customer Preference for
this potential buyer at your Make-or-Break
Moment if you want to grow your revenue.*

You now have this potential customer within your grasp. How do you determine what he really wants to buy and, more important, what emotions are driving his purchase decision? When you discover his state of mind concerning this purchase, you will be able to exert your influence and persuade this prospective customer to buy from you instead of your competitors.

Satisfying the Buyer's Need for Independence

As explained in the previous chapter, the customer's need for independence is one of the prime buyer behavioral changes that confront sellers today. To win this customer who treasures her independence, you must understand what independence means to buyers in the current buyer-seller context. It could mean any of the following:

- Being personally immersed in the discovery of the product or service

- Being confident of her knowledge

- Being in a position to compare, select, negotiate, and decide for herself

- Being in control

- Being free from pressure to buy the product or service she wants rather than the product or service the seller wants her to buy

- Being free from pressure to buy anything at all

- Being sought after, catered to, and accommodated

- Being in the "game" of buying and enjoying a "victory" in this "game," however small

These aspects of the psychology behind buyer independence illustrate its importance in the creation of Customer Preference at your Make-or-Break Moment. You must be sensitive to this pivotal change in buyer behavior as you prepare for the highly independent buyer whom you want to persuade to buy from your firm.

But one important buyer attribute has not changed. This buyer—*yes, even this very independent buyer*—feels vulnerable when she is in the process of purchasing something important to her. This buyer needs your help and advice, because she has an intense desire to make the right decision.

The contradiction of buyer independence and buyer vulnerability creates a new, profoundly important role for sellers to play during the prolonged Make-or-Break Moment.

The seller's new role is customer engagement.

In the context of today's buyer-seller equation, "engagement" means substantive interaction and involvement, but it does not mean codependency. These independent buyers do not want sellers to be aggressive and arrogant, nor do they want sellers to be passive and uninvolved, nor are they looking for a lifelong friendship. They want, expect, and demand the seller's attentiveness, expertise, and service when it benefits them most—*at their decisive moment of purchase*. They want sellers to offer them benefits that include but extend well beyond financial benefits. They want sellers to offer them meaningful solutions that directly relate to their wants, needs, and aspirations and to their apprehensions, concerns, and fears.

When buyers—even those buyers who feel empowered and in control most of the time—are in their purchasing phase, they seek and welcome the sellers' engagement. "Do I like and trust this seller better than other sellers?" is the fundamental question that's always running through buyers' heads. Buyers initially assess sellers' abilities and willingness to deliver this engagement at their first point of contact, but it becomes a crucial factor in their decision to move through the extended consideration, negotiation, and transaction phase. This is why most transactions are such a long process and why you have a valuable opportunity to create Customer Preference at the Make-or-Break Moment.

You can create Customer Preference at your Make-or-Break Moment by demonstrating that you will remain consistently engaged.

However, the moment your ability to engage your prospect stops, you will most likely lose the sale.

The Low (or No) Cost of Engagement

If you are willing to change your behavior to adapt to your buyer's changed behavior, engagement will enable you to consistently create Customer Preference at your Make-or-Break Moment.

Arguably the greatest merchant who ever lived, Stanley Marcus, who transformed Neiman Marcus into an international fashion icon, understood and practiced the art of engaging customers. Rather than sit in his office, he would roam the store, welcoming and engaging prospects and big spenders alike.

Moreover, when someone was trying on an extravagant fur coat or a brilliant diamond and ruby necklace or an outrageously expensive ball gown, Stanley would suddenly "appear out of nowhere" (secretly summoned by his well-trained staff). Of course, he would take the opportunity to compliment the customer's preference for a particular fur, necklace, or gown and mention, "It looks like it was made for you." In a well-practiced routine, the salesperson would quietly step away to select additional expensive items that might supplement and complement the merchandise the customer had finally selected. Stanley would usually offer a comment that the complementary merchandise looked particularly attractive with the fur, necklace, or gown. Stanley would frequently transform this buyer's simple shopping trip into a large, profitable selling occasion for Neiman Marcus. He was the grand master of customer engagement.

Those of us who are not Stanley Marcus can become very effective at customer engagement and can train our staffs to be effective as well. Engaging customers is one of the least expensive things we can do to further the sales process. And it might save us substantial time and lost revenue by potentially shortening the sales cycle and curbing price negotiations. Engagement can often offset a price reduction from an overeager competitor, and it often generates positive word of mouth and referrals from customers because it is a tangible demonstration of their smart choice.

Sellers must simply follow these rules of customer engagement.

Rules of Customer Engagement

- Engagement is not the buyer's job, it is the seller's job.

- Engagement doesn't just happen—it must be *made to happen*. It must be a practiced discipline, and training is essential. However, it must be delivered in a genuine, personal, and trustworthy manner.

- Engagement must not be interrupted by other business issues, other customer involvement, or any other distractions—the buyer wants to feel that he or his firm is the only star in the galaxy.

- Engagement that's backed up by something in writing—a warranty, a phrase in the contract, a letter from management, or a card with your home number—is more valuable than a handshake or a promise.

- Engagement from a senior executive is far more valuable than from the salesperson the customer is dealing with.

- Engagement is a valuable selling asset, but engagement alone is not enough to create Customer Preference—the customer must believe that he is getting the best product or service from the transaction.

- Engagement without fulfillment is both dangerous and counterproductive.

I had a speaking engagement in Boston, and the venue suggested several nearby hotels. I searched online and narrowed my choice to a Hilton and a Sheraton. I emailed each to inquire about its availability, rates, and fitness center.

The Sheraton seemed best, but its fitness center did not open until seven a.m. and I needed access at five a.m. to get a workout in before my speech. I called the Sheraton to see if I could get early access to its gym, and the person on duty at the reception desk said that she would talk to the manager about my needs and get back to me. Within the hour, I received a personal email from the manager, who said that early access was not available for security reasons but that he would place a stationary bike in my room without extra cost. I booked the Sheraton immediately because the manager had listened closely to my concerns and provided an imaginative solution that was very valuable to me but cost him very little. This engagement from the seller created Customer Preference at my decisive Make or Break Moment of transaction!

How to Engage Customers to Create Customer Preference

Following is a list of fairly common buyer wants and needs at the purchase decision moment. Some might seem insignificant and others might seem excessive, but each is valuable to some potential customer and each offers an opportunity for the seller to be engaged and to create Customer Preference at the Make-or-Break Moment.

- Can you deliver it on Thursday between two p.m. and four p.m.?
- Can you make it with blue stripes to match my curtains?
- Can you get my shipment to Singapore by September 1?
- Can you have my tux refitted for my son's wedding the day after tomorrow?
- Can you give me a corner room on a high floor with a view of the ocean?
- Can you throw in a GPS for the same price?
- Can you comply with my company's payment terms?
- Can you drop ship to my stores now that I've closed my warehouse?
- Can you respond to my RFP today (my boss leaves town tomorrow)?
- Can you repair this without cost (by the way, the warranty just expired)?
- Can you translate my presentation slides into Korean by six p.m. today?
- Can you get me back online for my Skype conference call in two hours?
- Can you give me a green interior in my new car rather than blue?

Would you engage with your potential customer to find a good solution to one or more of these wants or needs?

Make no mistake—this is not a call for sellers' submission to buyers.
But your transaction may very well hang in the balance over a
want or a need your potential customer finds valuable when she
is trying to choose between you and several aggressive competitors. If you are not fully engaged at the Make-or-Break Moment,
you will miss out on an opportunity to fulfill your prospect's
needs and will provide one of your competitors with the opportunity to make that firm the buyer's 1st choice instead.

To engage your customers and discover their emotional con-
siderations so that you can use them to create Customer Preference, follow these tips:

- Remember that every purchaser buys on emotion as well
  as the functionality or price of the product or service being
  sold pitch your product or service in the context of the
  prospect's needs and apprehensions, consistent with the
  customer-centric business model.

- Never start your interaction, verbal or otherwise, with
  information about your business. That is proof that you are
  thinking like a seller, not thinking like the buyer you are
  trying to win. Your credentials are not relevant until and
  unless you demonstrate that you can address the prospect's
  needs or anxieties. This is the path to engagement. Moreover, beginning with your credentials will not capture your
  prospect's attention or differentiate your firm, because this
  is probably what your competition will do, too.

- Start by identifying the prospect's challenge or problem
  from your perspective, because this will demonstrate that
  you have done your homework and will generate questions

from your prospect. Yes, it can be risky to lead with something that is provocative, but from my experience, this idea is less risky than not engaging the prospect.

- At the right time, proceed with your generalized solution to the prospect's problem or, even better, your specific imaginative solution to the challenge. I can almost guarantee that the seller with the best, most innovative solution to the prospect's problem, regardless of other factors, will win, because that is what the prospect is hungry for. Customer Preference and a single, clearly articulated, imaginative idea will win the day.

- Conclude with the primary reason that your firm is uniquely qualified to provide the solution rather than with a litany of capabilities. Your firm's credentials can be described briefly in a send-ahead or leave-behind or can be addressed later when it seems appropriate; however, today's buyers, having done their own Internet research, probably know a great deal already about your firm.

- Provide ample time for answering the prospect's questions, as this is your best opportunity to create engagement and Customer Preference.

- If you have been dealing with a gatekeeper, as described in the previous chapter, carefully encourage your contact to get you to the decision maker early in the firm's purchasing process, or your competitor will get there before you. You should be focusing your efforts on engaging the decision maker.

- Going around the gatekeeper is suicide. So if you are skillful enough or lucky enough to get through the gate and to the decision maker, think about bringing in someone who can engage the gatekeeper so that you are free to establish a relationship with the decision maker without alienating your original contact.

Converting a prospect into a customer also requires vigilance. Your competitors have not given up: They're still trying to persuade your prospect that they—not you—are the place to buy. They may be offering your prospect one or more of those things you refuse to provide. And to make matters worse, they may be bad-mouthing you, something you should never do because it usually backfires. Remain alert to the competitive threat throughout your lengthy transaction phase, and continue to create Customer Preference—it's the only antidote to the competitive challenge during the transaction progression.

The Art of Customer Engagement in Practice

Brad Skelton is the director of Skelton Sherborne, a company that specializes in shipping heavy machinery around the world. I hope that his interesting, rewarding customer engagement experience, told in his own words and used with his permission, will give you a real appreciation for the role of customer engagement in creating Customer Preference:

> In February 2001 Foot and Mouth Disease (FMD) broke out in the United Kingdom and rapidly spread across

Europe and other parts of the world. This highly contagious disease was devastating to the livestock industry. In the United Kingdom alone over 10 million cattle and sheep were slaughtered in an attempt to stop the spread. Apart from transferring from animal to animal, FMD can also be spread in soil and stay dormant there for years.

Skelton Sherborne specializes in shipping heavy machinery around the globe. This includes used and new earthmoving, mining, construction, and agricultural machinery for some of the leading manufacturers, dealers, and contractors worldwide. The equipment that is used is contaminated with soil, and when FMD broke out, we literally had hundreds of used machines on the water heading for Australia and New Zealand.

The fact that Australia and New Zealand are island nations has made them relatively safe from biological threats and pests commonly found elsewhere. Both countries depend heavily on agriculture, so their governments have long maintained the toughest quarantine regulations in the world to protect the local industry and the environment.

So when the largest FMD outbreak in history occurred, how did they react? Australian and New Zealand quarantine authorities immediately put in place a stringent inspection program for all used equipment arriving on their shores, and the government gave them the authority to order re-export, at the importer's expense, if the slightest trace of any contaminated soil was found.

This created a catastrophe for our customers and our own company. Machines were arriving and being sent straight back out, and the financial injury to all involved was enormous. No compensation was available to the importer from the governments, which defended their right to protect local industry from FMD however they saw fit.

Consequently, our customers lost confidence in importing machinery, and we could see our own market being rapidly decimated by this crisis. Everyone was losing. We had to find a way to give our customers the confidence they needed to keep importing without fear of re-export due to soil contamination.

We set about headhunting former Australian and New Zealand quarantine officers to join our team. The plan was to fly them all over the world, inspecting and washing the equipment to meet quarantine standards before it was loaded on board the ships. We initially did this on a cost recovery basis to help our customers and in turn help us keep moving the equipment. While our customers found the whole thing an expensive inconvenience, they knew that the quarantine commission was acting in the country's best interests and appreciated that we had reacted and delivered a solution. The bottom line was that we stemmed and eventually stopped the flow of re-exports. The whole market soon embraced our new innovative service. Our customers loved us, and our competitors were floundering and trying to play catch up.

The FMD crisis that confronted our clients, our company, and our industry presented an opportunity for us to take the lead among the tribe of people affected by the FMD crisis in Australia and New Zealand. We acted as advocates for our clients with the quarantine commission, asking for relaxation of the formalities as the FMD problem subsided. We are recognized to this day as the people you need to have working for you if you have problems with quarantine.

Here are other examples of business leaders who created Customer Preference by engaging customers—some are small personal gestures, and others demonstrate significant personal engagements.

One of my clients is a leading regional provider of kitchen installations—new kitchens as well as remodeled kitchens. Like many industries, this is a highly competitive category. There are high-quality, reliable suppliers (such as my client) and low-quality, bait-and-switch vendors. The range of materials, designs, installation techniques, and product durability confuses potential customers, making the customer's decision process difficult and frustrating. My client, a family-owned business, was effectively employing family members during the transaction process. However, the firm's conversion scores were not as high as it wanted, and when it went toe-to-toe with the cut-price firms, it reduced its margins. This kitchen cabinet seller needed to create Customer Preference at its Make-or-Break Moment.

Here was the firm's engaging solution: It invested in an impressive, user-friendly showroom where customers could see, feel, and understand the firm's wide range of options, high-quality standards, and installation rigor. A family member, stationed at the showroom, reinforced the family's dedication to performance for customers. The company's conversion scores and margins improved dramatically with this engagement at the purchasing decision. In a high-anxiety decision category, customer engagement will create Customer Preference at the Make-or-Break Moment.

Another client specializes in international motor sports marketing—its customers are committed to multiyear, multimillion-dollar contracts that involve everything from sponsorships of driving teams to brand identification on helmets and cars to dealer events at racetracks. This niche involves a high-anxiety purchase decision, especially for customers who are unfamiliar with the popularity and promotion benefits of motor sports.

Here is how my client engages the decision maker at the Make-or-Break Moment: It invites this senior executive to a big race—such as the Indy 500. The potential customer experiences the thrill of the sport, witnesses the huge crowds, and meets famous drivers and industry personalities. This engaging experience produces Customer Preference at this firm's Make-or-Break Moment.

When my company was interviewing technology firms to keep our hardware and software functioning and up to date, each firm assured us that it would "be there for us." Like everyone else in the world, we cannot afford prolonged tech problems, so we drilled down deep on this key issue before selecting a resource. Of course, each firm trotted out its heavy hitter, but one top executive handed me his card and said, "My cell phone and home phone numbers are on the card, so feel free to contact me anytime our help desk is unable to fix your problem." There have been rare occasions when this was necessary, but his personal engagement reassured us at our moment of purchase.

Recently, I was purchasing some wine for a large business event. I told the salesperson that I seemed to be buying far more than I actually needed. The salesperson told his boss about my concern, and she came over to assure me that the store would take back all unused wine and refund me in full. It was clear to me that this salesperson was trained by the firm to involve his boss at this kind of occasion so she could be engaged at the firm's Make-or-Break Moment.

As you can see, engaging customers with personal gestures or impressive interventions can create Customer Preference at your Make-or-Break Moment. Here is the good news—this engagement that buyers value so much usually costs sellers little or nothing to provide.

Today's buyer has done his homework, has chosen the "finalists" to consider, and is ready to buy. *When services or products from competitors are similar or even identical to yours, engagement will be the differentiator.* More often than not, this differentiator, this customer engagement, is the "value add" that creates Customer Preference at the profoundly decisive Make-or-Break Moment. Your next opportunity to sustain Customer Preference is your Keep-or-Lose Moment, the crucial period when customers are actually using the product or service they purchased from you.

Take a Moment to Consider...

how you can create preference at your Make-or-Break Moment.

1. Do you know your current prospect-to-customer conversion ratio? Do you consistently examine the trends in your conversation ratio? Accurate measurement and analytical analysis

of your prospect-to-customer conversion is essential. If you don't know how you are performing, you won't be able to set or achieve improvement in your conversion ratio.

2. Train your sales staff to exhibit patience and perseverance; the consideration, negotiation, and transaction process is often lengthy and usually dangerous. Today, the old-style selling techniques of pressure and dominance rarely generate sales. Your potential buyers value their independence and are looking for sellers who are willing to be their partners in the purchase progression.

3. Post the Rules of Customer Engagement (repeated, for your reference, on the next page) where your sales staff can see them every day. To optimize your conversion performance, you have to be engaged with your prospect in numerous small ways. Provide some valuable news about the product or service she is considering buying from you, or send an email that's relevant to a cause he's interested in. Remember that Customer Preference is also about likability and trust and influencing customers when they are making emotion-based decisions. If your transaction is expensive or complex, or if there is some urgency or anxiety involved, look for a way to be engaged in a big way.

4. Establish a clear policy of concessions and ways to wow prospects that will turn them into customers. How many customer requests have you said no to in the last two months? Is there a policy change you could make that might increase your conversion ratio while costing your business very little money? Don't get bogged down in old practices that aren't meeting the needs of modern customers.

Many things can go wrong at your Make-or Break Moment— your priority task is to assure that many things go right.

6

KEEP-OR-LOSE—THE CUSTOMER'S CONTINUED USAGE

It is the most overlooked opportunity in business.

Your customer has paid for your product or service and is now using, consuming, driving, wearing, talking on, practicing with, or surfing on it. Most important of all, your customer is relying on it. Now—when your product or service is paramount with your customer—is the best time to reinforce the Customer Preference you created during the purchase progression. This often-overlooked action costs little or nothing and will help you generate repeat purchase and advocacy from this customer. Compare your modest effort and expense to *retain* this valuable customer with your considerable effort and expense to *secure* a new customer, and you'll understand why your Keep-or-Lose Moment is so important to your company's bottom line.

"Customer churn" is the most common and most destructive cause of bottom line shrinkage.

During your customer's prolonged usage period—the decisive Keep-or-Lose Moment—you must achieve three objectives:

1. Ensure that your customer is benefiting from your product or service, that performance expectations are met or exceeded, and that the service and support you promised are being delivered.

2. Communicate with your customer from time to time to keep your company or brand uppermost in the customer's memory bank and demonstrate your personal commitment and involvement. There is no substitute for the seller's expression of interest in the customer's level of satisfaction.

3. Lay the groundwork for your customer to become a repeat buyer and advocate so that you can take advantage of your highly profitable Multiplier Moment.

Far too many business leaders do not follow through on each of these objectives at their Keep-or-Lose Moment. Despite their good intentions, they allow the daily grind of business and their ambition to win yet another new customer to interfere with their need to perform for, communicate with, and create preference among the customers they have already fought so hard to secure. When they fail to follow through—when they allow customer churn to erode their profits—they lose the potential to generate the highly profitable revenue that accrues from repeat purchase and customer referral.

The Keep-or-Lose Moment is your least expensive and most valuable opportunity to retain customers, generate repeat purchases, and motivate advocacy and referral.

Performance: The Undisputed Mission of Every Business

Without consistent performance for customers *after a sale is closed*—when the product or service is actually being used—a business is unsustainable, because this is the moment of truth in the battle to reduce customer churn. Yet many businesses cease to exist because they forget this core mission. Today, the firms that thrive are those that constantly deliver the performance that customers expect, deserve, and have paid for. In our new market reality, in which buyers have the power, you have to fulfill this primary seller obligation over the long term if you want to establish enduring Customer Preference for your brand or company.

As I've emphasized, the most important rule of creating Customer Preference—at any stage in the purchase progression and for companies of any size or industry—is to think like your buyer. Here is a personal experience I had recently at a bank that did not think like a buyer, failed to perform at the level I expected as a customer, and therefore lost a long-term customer.

I went to a nearby branch of my bank to get rid of some small but annoying monthly charges for services that I did not want or need. I told the branch manager my problem and showed him the useless charges that had suddenly started to appear on my statements. I explained that I had been a customer for a long time and that I kept a healthy balance. He looked me up on his computer and called his supervisor at the bank's headquarters. When he got off the phone, he acknowledged that I was a very valued customer but stated, "The charges cannot be eliminated due to the bank's new policies." I told him that the bank's response was unacceptable and that I would move my account to another bank unless a solution was offered. He then said, "There is nothing I can do about it."

However, I, the buyer, could do something about it. I walked down the street to another bank where I learned that there would be no such charges and immediately moved my business. Later the same week I saw a TV commercial for my former bank. Its CEO played the starring role and intoned, "Our bank is dedicated to serving our customers."

How many companies—of every size and type—waste millions of dollars on advertising to bring in new customers, simply to replace the valuable customers they are losing every day by not thinking like a buyer and not performing to their expectations? That bank lost my business because it had forgotten to think the way a faithful customer thinks; it ignored my wants and needs. To make matters worse, it never tried to repair our relationship or persuade me to remain a customer. Focusing all of your energy on bringing in new customers and doing little to keep your existing customers happy is a straight path to defeat in the market.

Sharper Image had cool, cute, and seemingly well-designed products. It was almost impossible to walk by the store without something catching your eye and pulling you in (the company nailed the Now-or-Never Moment), and even harder to walk out without buying a gadget or even a big-ticket item branded with the then-famous and -respected Sharper Image name (it aced the Make-or-Break Moment). Over time, however, I bought two products—an air freshener and a hair clipper—and neither product functioned as promised. When I returned the air freshener for a refund, the clerk said, "We've had a lot of complaints about this model." Why were they still selling it if the performance was subpar? I trashed the hair clipper in a hotel in Hong Kong soon after buying it.

In 2008, Sharper Image filed for bankruptcy and closed all its stores. Sharper Image is just one of the many businesses that failed because the company did not deliver consistent customer performance, losing out on the invaluable customer benefit that performance creates. Even worse, Sharper Image did not seem to care whether its products met its customers' expectations. It neglected an opportunity to reduce customer churn—to convert customers into repeats and referrals—by doing nothing to communicate with its customers during usage of its products. Sharper Image was too busy trying to sell more products and too complacent, relying on the foot-traffic model to *attract* customers but not taking proper actions to *retain* customers. Sharper Image succeeded at the first point of contact and at the transaction moment, but it crashed at its usage moment.

Do not let his happen to you!

*Performance is the indispensable ingredient in
Customer Preference at the Keep-or-Lose Moment
and the undisputed mission of every enterprise.*

Sharper Image still exists as a shadow of its former prominence—with a handful of employees. Its new plan is to license products, brand them, and sell them through third-party retailers such as OfficeMax and Best Buy, relying on the brand recognition it spent years building. The tagline on its new site reads, "A new era of quality, innovation and design." This time around, the company must actually follow through on that promise of performance.

BMW, a long-time client of my advertising agency, thrives on its reputation for performance. This company knows that Customer Preference *is* its business. When BMW assigned us the advertising for its pre-owned cars, we spent a lot of time listening to BMW owners. We heard things like "I love my BMW," "I will never drive anything but a BMW," and "The only person who cares as much about the BMW I own is my service manager at BMW." It was then that we decided to market the pre-owned BMWs in contrast to *the competitors' new cars* rather than *the competitors' used cars.* This idea was a huge success because a large number of upscale car buyers—knowing that BMW consistently performs for the customer throughout the life of the product—were more interested in owning a pre-owned BMW than a new car by almost any other brand. This reflected BMW owners' Customer Preference for the BMW brand they purchased, drove, and adored—a result of the company's focus on lasting performance.

Success at the Keep-or-Lose Moment starts and ends with performance, because creating and maintaining Customer Preference during the usage of a product or service is impossible if the performance doesn't live up to the customer's expectations.

Performance must be the paramount mission of your company.

Performance through Customer Engagement

Customer engagement works in every category and every part of the world. For instance, in its attempt to penetrate the modern luxury bus market in India, Volvo supplied nearly twenty subsidized trial buses to a select group of operators in 2001. According to Financialtimes.com/Management, "The first step was to imprint on [them] that Volvo's promise of after-sales service was more than just words . . . When something went wrong, [the trainee riding on that bus] would immediately report to [the managing director], allowing him to quickly deploy a service unit to the stricken vehicle." Volvo was allowing the operators to "forgo the usual investment in workshops and maintenance facilities" and instead focus on "selling tickets" (Joe Leahy, "Volvo Takes a Lead in India," August 31, 2009).

Alistair Wandesforde is a partner with AW Systems, a technology consulting, global networking, and hosting company. In the following story, which he graciously allowed me to include here, he describes in his own words how his company offered superior performance and an imaginative solution by being engaged with its clients:

A few years ago, we offered our clients email and site hosting at no extra charge. Why would we do this? Our public stance was that we did it to create "stickiness" with our clients. Internally, we knew it would be easier to maintain control and troubleshoot problems if we had full access to our clients' sites and email systems. In our minds, it was a win-win situation—until the spam hit the fan.

Dealing with email-borne threats, such as spam and viruses, was nothing new; we had been doing it for years. However, the game changed in 2007, when there was an exponential growth of spam and viruses worldwide. At one point, there was a new virus popping up daily!

Managing the threats and sorting through the quarantined mail had become a full-time operation for our entire staff. Since email hosting was a part of our service, we could not bill these hours to the client, and our clients were losing valuable time waiting for us to filter through everything. We were sinking . . . fast.

The enormity of this task was compounded by our diverse client base, which made implementing global filters iffy at best. For example, an email with the keywords "breast" or "young beauties" would be highly inappropriate for our nonprofit theater client to find in its inbox, but could be a very legitimate message for our plastic surgeon or beauty product clients to receive.

If we could not find a solution, we were going to have to assign one person internally per client to analyze the daily pile of quarantined emails and help users manage their spam. Since this was not a realistic option, especially if we wanted to stay in business, we dug in and searched for a low-cost (since we were paying for it ourselves), highly effective tool to help us out of this mess.

After weeks of research, we found ONE candidate and decided to jump in with both feet by testing the technology on our own email system first. To make a long story short, it rocked! Our next step was to test the service in the real world, so we asked three of our clients to give it a go. The results? All three companies were floored by the effectiveness of the service and felt indebted to us for providing it at no extra cost to them.

Shortly thereafter, we rolled the service out to every one of our clients. Thanks to this service, in one month alone, our filters caught over 1 million spam emails and viruses before they could reach our clients' inboxes, which accounted for close to 50 percent of the total inbound email traffic!

While the motivation behind finding the service was our own self-preservation, we ended up being able to offer our clients a better, more reliable service that did not cost them a dime. It feels good to be the hero!

AW Systems went above and beyond to stay engaged with its customers and ensure that they were benefiting from the services the firm provided. But you can stay engaged with your customers using much less complex techniques. A personalized—not boilerplate—email or brief phone call to inquire about the customer's satisfaction is a simple, no-cost way to assure that your customer is benefiting from your product or service.

Recovering from Performance Failure

In Chapter 4, I offered some practical tips for dealing with a customer interaction that had gone poorly. The most important piece of that discussion is the concept that you must anticipate this situation, prepare for it, and train for it. Smart sellers understand that despite our best efforts, some customers will not be satisfied with our products and services. Whether this reaction is real or perceived, how you handle your performance failures will say more to your customers about how customer-centric you are than almost any other experience they have with you. Here are some tips to consider when you are faced with a performance problem:

- Be customer-centric and think like your buyer; she feels that you have failed to meet her expectations, so now you need to exceed them to remedy the situation.

- Listen carefully to the customer's complaint; the nuances of the complaint will help you understand why her expectations were not met and then turn the situation around.

- Be apologetic—sincerely apologetic.

- Express your desire to try once again to meet her expectations.

- Ask the customer what would make her happy, and then do your best to go beyond that expectation; if the customer's expectation is unrealistic, explain why you can't fulfill that desire, but identify all the other ways that you could remedy the situation. Always have an arsenal of options available to help you resolve a customer complaint, because every customer will have different expectations.

The hospitality industry has more opportunities for success and failure to perform and create preference than any other industry, because it has more points of customer contact. Think about it—booking, check-in, food service, housekeeping, wake-up calls, fitness centers, luggage handling, bill preparation, checkout, etc. I write about this industry quite often because these are situations that readers have actually experienced and find relevant to their industry or firm, even if it is in a very different category.

Here are two very different personal experiences that illustrate both success and failure at the Keep-or-Lose Moment.

To recover from performance failure,
deliver performance in another way.

My plane arrived in Austin an hour late, and I needed to get to my hotel to freshen up before a dinner engagement with my publisher. I called the Marriott that my client had recommended to ask that the hotel send its van to pick me up at the airport as quickly as possible. I went to the designated pickup spot, and after a very long wait, I contacted the hotel again. The person on duty admitted that there had been confusion at that end and suggested that I grab a taxi and the hotel would pay for it. A good example of trying to recover from performance failure, I thought—an honest explanation and a quick, smart solution.

My taxi arrived at the Marriott, and I rushed to the reception desk to check in. In a matter of seconds, the manager appeared and apologized for the delay at the airport. He immediately paid the taxi fare and told me that he was putting four thousand Marriott points in my Marriott Rewards account.

I thanked him and hurried off to my room. Soon after the elevator door closed, a message came through on my BlackBerry, telling me that four thousand Marriott points had arrived in my Marriott Rewards account. I was a little late for my dinner but had time to be impressed with the manager's performance at his Keep-or-Lose Moment. A prompt, sincere apology and an immediate, generous solution established Customer Preference for this Marriott property. I now stay at this Marriott on each trip to Austin.

To recover from performance failure is to acknowledge the failure and rectify it.

I had to go to London on business, and the airlines, given the impact of the economy, were offering rock-bottom prices. The fares were so affordable that my wife could come along with me. My wife went online to find a hotel that would be special but affordable. She found a recently remodeled, highly rated hotel in a great location at a great price—four nights for the price of three, with breakfast and VAT tax absorbed by the hotel. We booked the accommodations online and printed the hotel's offer from its site for our trip file.

A few days later, I received the hotel confirmation by email. My wife noticed that our room rate was higher because the VAT was added to the quoted rate. It was a sizable amount—moreover, it was inconsistent with the hotel's offer. I called the hotel about the matter and was referred to the headquarters of the hotel chain, where we were told that the VAT offer was no longer valid and that the current site reflected this change. Fortunately, the original offer and the date appeared on our printout. Our contact asked that we fax or scan the printout. Within a few hours, we received a corrected confirmation without the VAT and a note of apology saying that we had been upgraded to a better room because of the inconvenience. This performance—despite the extra effort it required on our part—at the hotel's Keep-or-Lose Moment was more than enough to create Customer Preference after an initial performance failure.

Being Top-of-Mind at Your Keep-or-Lose Moment

Being top-of-mind is not about "brand recall." After all, you and I "recall" such brands as Sharper Image, Circuit City, Pontiac, and any number of other companies that have disappeared or that are just hanging on. "Brand recall" means simply remembering the brand name or company name   it is not enough. Being top-of-mind, on the other hand, means that your customer remembers

- what your brand stands for,
- the benefits your brand or company provides while he is using the product, and
- how your brand performs for him as he uses it.

Being your customer's top-of-mind brand in your category is a great deal more valuable than just remembering the brand name. After all, Joe and Sue are just names, and these names do not tell you anything about Joe and Sue.

You want to become and remain your customer's top-of-mind brand or company in your category.

Being topmost means occupying a large space in the mind of your customer—a mind that is already crowded with brands the customer recalls but does not value. You want to push those other brands to the sidelines and own the space that houses the very few brands the customer values—the brands that deliver performance.

If you want your firm to remain your customer's 1st choice after the sale, you must deliver performance and create preference during the customer's usage.

Here is a great example of a B2B that understands the importance of occupying a large space in the customer's mind and pushing the competitive brands to the sidelines. It illustrates the value of

- establishing what the brand stands for,

- highlighting the benefits the seller provides to customers when the services are being used or may be used again, and

- providing information of real value to the customer's decision makers.

These are the essential elements of communicating in a way that will help you reinforce your high performance standards and maintain your top-of-mind presence with your customers.

You met Brad Skelton, director of Skelton Sherborne, in Chapter 5 when he described his engagement experience at the Make-or-Break Moment. Now you will see how Brad continues to build Customer Preference at his decisive Keep-or-Lose Moment.

Recently, Brad launched a blog—The Shipping Bloke. No, it is not just more "blah-blah-blah" and "seller talk." It is a carefully constructed, no-cost communications initiative that underscores the company's commitment to performance and creates top-of-mind awareness for the firm. His catchy nickname and blogsite remind the customer what services his company offers (shipping, of course), where the company is located (Australia, home of "blokes"), and what added value the company delivers to its customers—valuable, topical news about shipping heavy equipment.

For instance, in one blog posting Brad predicted changes in the liability regimes governing international shipping, provided insights about the new Rotterdam Rules, and offered some expert opinions about the advantages and disadvantages of this new convention as it affects the firm's customers. This stuff may not be important to you and me, but to Brad's customers, who are highly dependent on reliable heavy shipping services, this is mission-critical information.

In "So What If Deck Cargo Is Cheaper?" posted August 6, 2009, Brad was transformed into an iconic sage of the shipping industry with this gutsy message: "I rarely, if EVER, load heavy machinery on the deck of vessels . . . There literally has to be no other way to get the cargo to that destination before I will even vaguely consider it. Even then, I do my level best to make my client completely aware of the risks, accept them, notify their underwriters, and protect the cargo as much as possible."

Brad goes on to admit that he has frequently lost business to competitors who came in cheaper, precisely because they were taking risks with their clients' cargo. Says he, "I'd rather not handle the shipment than risk damaging the cargo—and my relationship with my customer with it." When a customer sees this kind of frankness and passion from a shipping firm, chances are pretty good that he will contact the Shipping Bloke.

*Communicating with customers in the
right way will keep you top-of-mind.*

Another client reinforces Customer Preference at the Keep-or-Lose Moment in a more flamboyant way. To remain top-of-mind, my upscale jewelry store client invites customers and their guests, usually important prospects, to lavish events at seasonal gift-giving moments.

Guests are encouraged to wear the merchandise they purchased from this jeweler to this preference-building event, and they are proud to show it off. These invitation-only events feature a jewelry designer, a famous jewelry authority, or a new jewelery supplier to add interest and appeal. My client welcomes her guests, introduces the vendor (who does not charge the store for his or her appearance), and encourages the attendees to enjoy the elaborate foods and beverages displayed in the theme of the particular gift-giving occasion, such as Christmas or Valentine's Day. Of course, the must-sign guest book captures names, the all-important email addresses, birth dates, and anniversary dates, enabling the store to create additional Customer Preference by mail or email on these special occasions.

Creating an occasion that is a "stage" for a firm's products reinforces Customer Preference and maintains the company's top-of-mind position. It is just one more way to achieve success at the Keep-or-Lose Moment.

When you consistently perform for and remain top-of-mind with customers at your Keep-or-Lose Moment, you are reinforcing Customer Preference right when they are using and benefiting from your product or service. *This is the time that is most important to the customers.*

It is also the time that is most important to you. At this highly influential and decisive moment, you are also laying the groundwork to transform your customers into repeat buyers, advocates, and enthusiastic referral sources. Preparing your customers to want to do business with you again (and again) and to help you prosper is how you compound the return on your efforts and investments, to establish Customer Preference throughout the purchase progression.

You will find out all about the techniques to use at your Multiplier Moment in Chapter 7.

Take a Moment to Consider...
how you can create preference at your Keep-or-Lose Moment.

1. Is customer churn eating your bottom line? If so, it is probable that your firm or your product is failing to meet customer expectations. Your priority must be to assure the best possible performance for customers after they have purchased your product or service.

2. Do you track customer complaints? Do you examine trends in those complaints? Most important, do you have a clear policy for handling performance failures? Having failed to meet a customer's expectations, you must now exceed them to retain the

Customer Preference you have created. Too many bad things can occur during your valued customer's usage of your product or service, and you may not discover the performance failure in time to rescue the relationship. Worse, your customer may spread the word about your failure over the back fence or on Facebook or Twitter. You must do whatever is possible to assure that this does not happen to you.

3. Reinforce Customer Preference by communicating with your customers while they are using the product, maintaining your top-of-mind ranking with those customers to avoid being forgotten and prevent competitors from capturing your invaluable favored status. If you do not communicate with customers, they will probably forget about your very existence, creating an opportunity for your competitor to get back in the door, outperform you, and become the customer's preferred resource. Frequent communication is a sound foundation on which to build repeat purchase and referral.

To ensure that you have the potential to generate repeat purchase, advocacy, and referral, don't overlook the most overlooked opportunity in business—creating Customer Preference at your Keep-or-Lose Moment.

7

THE MULTIPLIER—REPEAT PURCHASE, ADVOCACY, AND REFERRAL

Now is your chance to reap the rewards of your investment in creating Customer Preference.

The Multiplier Moment is the successful conclusion to your customer's purchase progression and your return on investment from all your hard work during the three Decisive Customer Moments that preceded it. It is this highly profitable moment—the solution to your customer churn problem—when your customer buys again (and again); advocates for you; and refers you to business associates, friends, family, and anyone who seeks a product or service like yours.

*At this Decisive Customer Moment, you
will generate multiple sales from your
investment in a single customer—a customer
for whom your firm is 1st choice.*

To secure this highly profitable new revenue at your Multiplier Moment, you must achieve four goals. Note that the first two are identical to two goals at your Keep-or-Lose Moment because they remain essential to your success at the Multiplier Moment.

1. Continue to assure that your customer receives consistent performance. Of all your too-numerous responsibilities, customer performance is paramount—it remains the priority mission of every business leader because performance is what your customer wants, expects, and has paid for. *Be obsessed with performance for your customers.*

2. Continue to communicate with your customer to maintain top-of-mind awareness. To be your customers' preferred resource—the firm they patronize often and recommend to others—your customer must think of your firm before any other firm when using your product or service or when contemplating a purchase of another product or service that you offer. Your customer is always tempted to try a new brand, to consider a new way of working, or to be receptive to a highly persuasive appeal from your hungry competitor. If you do not occupy the largest space in your customer's mind, some competitor will take your place.

3. Use your personal equity with your customer to motivate her to buy more and more often from you.

4. Use your personal equity with your customer to motivate her to advocate for you and refer you to those businesses and/or individuals she can influence.

Your personal equity with your customers is the source of opportunity to expand your revenue from customers and gain their advocacy and referral.

Your Personal Equity with Customers Is Valuable

Personal equity with a customer is built on the aggregate investments you made throughout the customer's prolonged purchase progression: the creation of Customer Preference at first contact with your firm, the frequent engagements with the customer, the consistent performance you delivered to the customer, and the top-of-mind awareness you maintained with the customer. When you make this commitment, you will have developed a bank of personal equity with the customer—personal equity that you can and must leverage to your advantage.

Many business leaders do not use, or they misuse, their personal equity with customers. Personal equity is much like financial equity—it is extremely valuable because it can generate highly profitable revenue from the customer's repeat purchase, advocacy, and referral.

Moreover, as with financial equity, you must employ personal equity wisely and carefully to realize the return on your investment. If your firm does not fully benefit from your efforts to establish Customer Preference and provide customer performance, you will be leaving this currency on the table.

What Personal Equity Is and Is Not

Personal equity is a highly valuable currency, not a currency of modest or little value. It is substantive and precious, and it is yours alone—it can't be borrowed, lent, traded, transferred, or sold. Don't use your personal equity to get something insignificant; use it to get something of significance to your business, one (and only one) of the important things you want or need: namely, additional business from the customer, introductions to new customers, or recommendations you can use with prospects. Do not make multiple requests of a customer all at once.

Personal equity is earned—it is not a currency that your customer gives you. It is not a favor that your customer owes you—your customer has no obligation to you. You can't earn it on the golf course or at the bar—it is earned by delivering performance to the customer day after day and year after year. And it's not something that you're entitled to, no matter how great your performance. Like many things in life, you may not get what you earn or even what you deserve.

Personal equity is perishable. Customers' memories are short, and there can be reversals in your working relationship with the customer that wipe out your personal equity overnight. Your customer may move on, retire, or get fired. Moreover, your competitors may have their own personal equity with your customers and may be able to leverage a friendship, tennis match, or hunting trip to their advantage—unless you get there first and use your personal equity with the customer to get what you (and your competitors) seek. Use your personal equity with your customer or lose it.

Personal equity is earned—it is highly valuable and perishable, and it must be used to gain something from the customer that is also highly valuable.

How Do You Earn Personal Equity?

Personal equity can be earned by consistent performance over time, as illustrated by this example.

My company had a small assignment from a large, diverse B2B organization and wanted more. I met the new CEO at an industry function and arranged a lunch to get better acquainted, never asking for anything. When I was sure that we were performing for this client on our assignment and confident that I had gained the CEO's trust, I scheduled another lunch, promising myself to ask for another small assignment or two.

After our usual chitchat, I was about to pop the question when he said in a rather sober tone that he wanted to discuss business. Then he said, "We are not happy with our main agency relationship and have decided to make a change." I felt sure our small assignment was in jeopardy. Instead, he said the words that I will never forget: "We would like to move our entire account into one agency, and we hope you will give us the same kind of performance on all our lines of business as you are giving on the assignment you handle now." I was stunned but managed to blurt out something that I no longer remember.

Being persistent, sensitive, and patient while you earn personal equity can be very rewarding.

Personal equity can also be earned by a grand gesture. Brian Barker is the senior vice president and general manager of EmploymentGroup Managed Services (EGMS), which helps companies manage contracted services. EGMS is a company whose product is literally service. It offers a variety of non-core options to companies that have made strategic decisions to concentrate on the core of their business and to partner with a company that is expert in contracted services. Brian told me about this fascinating story some time ago, and he's allowed me to share it with you because it's such an outstanding example of employing personal equity on a grand scale:

> In our business relationships, the goal is to form a partner-ship with our clients so that we become an integrated and invaluable part of the organization. We offer no unique prod-uct that others cannot offer, and our competitors can and do make claims as to their expertise. Our point of differentiation is that we seek to be completely engaged and integrated.
>
> We are in a very competitive, niche business. Our teams are trained formally and extensively in customer service, and in our hiring, we seek out those who show a talent for relationship building.
>
> Our clients are signed for lengths of three to five years and at the end of the term, they go into the marketplace

and seek other companies to bid on the contract. As you may imagine, as the incumbent, we have everyone involved in the bid process shooting at us.

Our client in this example is a large, Midwestern, Division I school based in Kalamazoo, Michigan. Western Michigan University has a student population of about 24,000 and faculty in the thousands.

WMU has been a client with us for over ten years. We have gone through the bid process twice before and won each time. We were up for rebid at the end of 2008, and it was to be an open bid process.

Prior to the bid process, we had a situation that enabled us to engage our customer and make a substantive difference in the bidding process.

In the fall of 2008, work crews that were engaged in a major construction project at the WMU campus caused a rupture in the main waterline to the campus and dorms. This accident created an enormous problem for our customer, as there was no potable water for drinking or cooking, and no water for sanitation purposes. The nature of the break was such that the school would be unable to repair it for several days.

Our staff at WMU operates the mailroom and logistic services on campus, so were very familiar with the campus. We offered to help the university by providing the use of our trucks and vans to assist in this crisis.

Our account manager and his team used the equipment we had on-site to bring huge quantities of fresh water to several sites on campus and distribute it. They coordinated with the campus police and successfully distributed water until late that night and on the next day. This was a spontaneous effort—one that the team did without any thought to how this may affect our business relationship. Moreover, it was without additional compensation. Our staff simply recognized a problem and, as part of the campus community, made it happen.

Little did we know the effect this would have in our negotiations and the decision process of WMU. Two months later, we submitted our proposal along with five other competitors.

The criteria for WMU had many components, and low price was not the determining factor. I say this because we were not the low bid and yet our contract was renewed. They thought of us as a part of the fabric of the campus community and rewarded us for our day-to-day performance and this selfless engagement.

Capitalizing on circumstances that involve your customers can result in an exceptionally valuable grand gesture that creates personal equity.

How to Leverage Your Personal Equity to Gain More Business

I arranged a meeting with a long-term client, a division of a large drug products company with multiple business units and brands. At the end of our business conversation, I expressed appreciation for our positive working relationship and told him I was seeking an introduction to one of his company's other divisions.

I explained why my company was especially qualified to create advertising for the other division's brands and concluded with a reminder that if this made him uncomfortable I would understand and respect his decision.

Without commenting, he picked up the phone and contacted the president of the division I wanted to meet with. He made some positive comments about my agency and our work and asked her to let me stop by her office. I had a great meeting with the prospect, briefly outlined our capabilities, and answered her questions. She said that the time was not right for an agency change but that we would be one of the first agencies she would contact if future circumstances warranted a change.

Almost a year later, she called, and we won the business.

One of our clients was a global foods company. An executive of the company, whom I had met on several occasions, was named president of its unit in Australia. I continued to send him my periodic "Notes from Bob" that informed clients and prospects of interesting changes in the marketplace, our perspectives on new marketing techniques, and the progress of our agency.

Several years later, this individual returned to the U.S. organization as its CEO. Of course, I dropped him a note of congratulations and soon after arranged a lunch with him at the headquarters. During our luncheon conversation, he told me that my agency was the only ad agency that had maintained contact while he was overseas for five years. He and I became good friends and met often throughout his long, successful career.

Numerous new assignments from this firm came our way over the next few years, because of our performance as well as the top-of-mind awareness we had established in the corner office.

How to Leverage Your Personal Equity to Generate Referral and Advocacy

Referrals and advocacy can produce significant incremental sales, and because there is no cost associated with this initiative, it generates highly profitable new revenue. But generating referrals and advocacy from your customers does require finesse and patience.

Here are some guidelines to achieve success when you seek a referral from a current customer:

- Ask in person—never use email, mail, or the phone. Personal equity must be used in person or postponed until it can be done effectively in person.

- Be straightforward—at the outset, state that you value this customer's business and would never do anything to disrupt it. Then, use your personal equity—explain that you are seeking a referral.

- Always give the customer an opportunity to opt out—state early and firmly that you will understand and respect a decision not to make the referral if it is an inappropriate or uncomfortable request.

- Do not ask a customer for advocacy or referral more than once—if it does not happen in response to your first request, it will not happen at all (and you may have a performance problem with this customer if you persist).

- Thank your customer, and after your contact with the referral, provide your customer with immediate, candid feedback on the outcome—again expressing your appreciation.

- Make very sure that you perform for the customer's referral—otherwise, you jeopardize your relationship with your original customer.

Customers who benefit from your performance and prefer your firm are likely to be flattered that you asked them to help you.

Repeat Customers and Referred Customers Come with Great Expectations

There is nothing more important to a repeat customer than a warm welcome back when he returns to buy more from you.

If your internal systems aren't configured to prompt you when a customer returns, add this valuable systems component and use it to flatter a returning customer. No one does this better than the Four Seasons hotels and resorts do. When a repeat customer walks up to the reception desk to register, the receptionist takes a quick look at the prompt in the reservation and says, "Welcome back to the Four Seasons, Mr. Jones." Obviously, Jones is delighted and proud, especially if others checking in hear this personalized greeting.

This technique can be used in any type of firm—when your staff or systems alert you to a repeat customer, no matter how modest or frequent the repeat purchase, an email to the customer that expresses appreciation for her continued patronage will go a long way to reinforce Customer Preference.

In a world without customer loyalty, never miss an opportunity to welcome and reward a repeat customer.

Moreover, there are numerous ways to reward customers who patronize your firm. Here are just a few ways to make your most valuable customers feel special and appreciated:

- Provide them with early notification and early access to new products, services, or pricing.

- Offer the benefits of well-regarded reward programs, such as American Airlines' AAdvantage miles.

- Make a dedicated hotline available to them for immediate answers to questions and special assistance.

- Invite them to periodic special "thank-you events."

Be sure to let your most valued customers know that they, and they alone, are receiving these rewards.

Sellers must be just as diligent in how they handle referred customers. It's important to point out that customers who refer you are doing so because they value your contributions and respect you as a business associate. Customers will only refer you if your products or services have benefited them *and* you have earned their trust. *It's not one or the other—it's benefits as well as trust.*

Further, if your customer feels this strongly about you, she's not using her personal equity with her contact to get a gift from you—so don't create embarrassment for you or your customer by giving her a gift in connection with the referral. Many firms have policies that prevent the acceptance of gifts, and your customer doesn't want anything from you except your continued performance, your sincere expression of appreciation, and your performance for her referral that justifies the use of your personal equity with her. If it's been customary to give this customer a holiday gift or treat her to dinner, just make this occasion a little more special.

As discussed, referrals occur in abundance when customers are fully satisfied with your performance and when you have created Customer Preference for your firm, but be very aware that the person who has been referred to you will arrive with very high expectations. Expect this level of expectation, prepare for it, and meet or exceed the expectation so that the referral and your customer will not be disappointed or—far worse—feel betrayed.

If your current customer advises you in advance that a prospective customer will be contacting you, be fully prepared to create Customer Preference at first contact. However, this type of warning does not occur very often. All the more reason that, in those instances when the email, phone call, or visit from a referral is unexpected, you and your team must be ready to make your prospect's first contact a positive one. Any referral to your firm from a current customer is doubly important, because it can result in a gain of one new customer—or the loss of two sources of income if your prospect gives a negative report to the customer who referred you.

This happened to me once, but only once, in my long career in advertising. A valuable client in a different technology category referred a large technology marketer to us. When the prospect called, my associates with the most extensive B2B experience and I were traveling. Unfortunately, a colleague with limited B2B experience tried to outline our credentials to serve the prospect's highly specialized needs.

The prospect was not impressed with our capabilities as described to him and, as a result, the prospect eliminated our agency from further consideration. Our existing client was embarrassed and angry. Although I met with him and apologized, we never recovered from the incident, and not too long after it, he terminated us.

As you can see, meeting the high expectations of a referral can prove difficult. Here is the lesson:

Train your organization to make every Multiplier Moment a special, positive experience.

Make Your Multiplier Moment a Reality

Very few moments in business are more gratifying than gaining advocacy or a referral from a valued customer. Your personal equity is currency—use it, but use it smartly and carefully to make your Multiplier Moment a profitable reality.

You have become familiar with the need to think like a buyer and act like a seller, and you know how to use each of the 4 Decisive Customer Moments to make your business 1st choice. Now you are ready to put this methodology to work for your business. In the very brief final chapter, you will discover why you must move with a sense of urgency.

Take a Moment to Consider...

how you can create preference at your Multiplier Moment.

1. What measures do you have in place to track repeat purchase and referral? How do you handle clients when they return to buy more from your company? Do you continue to build Customer Preference, or are you losing out on the most valuable opportunity your business has? Investments in the customers you have are far more profitable than those made to attract new customers, so be smart about how you are spending your time, money, and efforts.

2. To help ensure that your customer purchases often from you, becomes an advocate, and generates referrals, you will need to leverage your personal equity with your customer. Of course, these three beneficial results may occur when your customer is well satisfied with his purchase from you. You can let this happen naturally and reap the rewards from it. But leveraging your personal equity will assure that repurchase, advocacy, and referral will happen.

3. Build personal equity by consistently creating Customer Preference with a customer and then going beyond. Use grand gestures, wow moments, and personal investment in the relationship with her to take your personal equity to the next level.

4. Train your staff explicitly on how to leverage their personal equity with customers. Don't let them lose an opportunity because they failed to take the equity they built and use it at the right time. If you don't use it when it's appropriate, you are almost certain to lose it—and lose an existing or potential customer.

Your valuable Multiplier Moment will occur when you take the right action at the right time with the right person. Use your personal equity or it will evaporate.

8

THE URGENCY TO MAKE YOUR BUSINESS 1ST CHOICE

Throughout this book, I have emphasized the need for each and every business leader to change the way he or she thinks and works.

However, talking about change is not the act of changing.

From my experience in the business trenches, I know that changing, however difficult, is the essential ingredient in enduring business success. I also discovered that change is rewarding—personally and professionally. You, too, will benefit personally and professionally from changing.

That need to change how you think and work is not only essential; it is also urgent.

Changing is urgent because your customers
have already changed how they think
and how they buy from you.

The change in customers' buying behavior was both swift and profound and has affected businesses all over the world, including your firm. Yet this change will seem modest by comparison with future changes in customers' desire and ability to control how they purchase and from whom they purchase.

The future will belong to companies and
brands that have an imaginative, disciplined,
customer-centric business model.

Just imagine how these two recent developments, still in their infancy, could affect your business in the future:

1. GM's exploration of an agreement with eBay to sell cars on the Web.

2. Digital Forming has developed technology that enables customers to "codesign" the interior of the Fiat 500, the style and fit of their Nike sneakers, and the colors of Ray-Ban Wayfarer sunglasses.

Technology will continue to empower your
customer to think and buy differently.

Customer loyalty is not hibernating, waiting for the right time to return. Customer loyalty is dead. This means that you must win over every customer time and time again by creating Customer Preference over and over again. Being customer-centric is not a temporary exercise; it is a permanent way of thinking and working. The revolution in buying behavior will continue to evolve and strengthen. Businesses of every size and type must play catch-up—fast.

Changing how you think and work is no longer an option. Reducing customer churn is no longer an option. Moving to a customer-centric business model is no longer an option. If you want your business to be your customer's 1st choice, you must create and sustain Customer Preference for your firm at all 4 Decisive Customer Moments.

You now know how to think like a buyer and act like a seller—do both now, before your competition does!